Understanding and Overcoming

Misophonia

A Conditioned Aversive Reflex Disorder

Thomas H. Dozier

Misophonia Treatment Institute, *Livermore, CA*

Understanding and Overcoming Misophonia:
A Conditioned Aversive Reflex Disorder

Published by Misophonia Treatment Institute
5801 Arlene Way
Livermore, CA 94550

ISBN 978-0-692-49482-0

Disclaimer

The information presented herein represents the views of the author as of the date of publication. This book is presented for informational purposes only. Due to the rate at which conditions change, the author reserves the right to alter and update his opinions at any time. While every attempt has been made to verify the information in this book, the author does not assume any responsibility for errors, inaccuracies, or omissions.

This book does not offer medical advice nor is it intended as a substitute for the medical advice of a physician. The reader should regularly consult a physician in matters relating to his/her health and particularly with respect to any symptoms that may require diagnosis or medical attention.

The names of patients who have provided testimonials have been changed to protect their privacy.

Contents

1. The Misophonia Experience 1

    Misophonia Triggers 6

    Misdiagnoses 7

    "My Misophonia" 8

2. Diagnosing Misophonia 10

    How to Determine if You Have Misophonia or Not 13

    Rating the Severity of Misophonia 13

        Misophonia Activation Scale (MAS-1) 14

        Amsterdam Misophonia Scale (A-MISO-S) 15

        Misophonia Assessment Questionnaire 19

3. Triggers, Triggers, and More Triggers 22

4. Oh, the Emotions! 25

    Misophonia Emotional Responses 25

5. Oh, the Guilt! 28

6. Prevalence of Misophonia 31

7. Diversity of Misophonia 34

    The Age of Onset 34

    The Individual Physical Reflex 37

8. Prognosis for Misophonia 39

9. Perception Versus Reality 41

    Involuntary Emotional Response 41

Benefits of Understanding the Misophonic Physical Reflex.....48

Identifying Your Physical Reflex...49

All the Steps 51

Summary..52

10. Human Reflexes 53

11. How Misophonia Develops...55

Misophonia – An Aversive Conditioned Reflex 58

12. How Triggers Spread..60

Minimize Your Response 62

13. Talking about Misophonia..65

14. Management Techniques...68

General Health and Wellness 68

Avoid and Escape Triggers 69

Family Trigger Management Plans 70

Add Sound to Your Environment and Ears.................................71

Audiologists - Misophonia Management Protocol.....................72

Help with Headphones 77

Earplugs and Noise Cancelling Headphones..............................82

Daily Muscle Relaxation Practice 84

Overview of PMR and Applied Relaxation............................85

Guidelines for Progressive Muscle Relaxation 88

No Threat, But Thank You..91

Attitude 93

504 Plan for Workplace and School Accommodations...........95

A Few Tricks with Technology 97

15. Treatments 99

   Progressive Muscle Relaxation and Applied Relaxation 99

   Neural Repatterning Technique (NRT) 102

      Counterconditioning the Misophonia Reflex 105

      Case Studies 107

      The Trigger Tamer Apps 114

   Hypnotherapy - SRT 119

   Psychosomatic Remediation Technique (PRT) 122

   CBT/DBT 124

   Neurofeedback 126

   Medication for Anxiety or Depression 128

   Tinnitus Retraining Therapy 128

   Blocking a Reflex 129

16. Treatments to Avoid 130

17. Misophonia and Children 132

   Two Types of Kids Develop Misophonia 132

   Developing the First Misophonia Trigger 134

   What's a Parent to Do? 135

18. Misophonia or Conditioned Aversive Reflex Disorder

(CARD) 138

Your Next Step 141

References 142

Citations 147

1. The Misophonia Experience

My Introduction to Misophonia

Friday, August 31, 2012. I was working as a parent coach when a mother contacted me asking for help with her difficult daughter and the disruption she was causing in their family. She explained the extreme behavior and her daughter's unusual hatred of the breathing and eating sounds of her parents. She said it was called "misophonia" and there was no treatment for it. It was like a lightbulb went on in my head. All of a sudden, my daughter's irrational complaining about my loud chewing made sense. My daughter had misophonia also. She was now an adult with her own children and one of them had misophonia also.

My retirement income supported me and I had extra time, so I decided to investigate misophonia. My training as a behavior specialist taught me that there were two general classes of human behavior. The first is purposeful behavior—the things we do. The second class of behavior is reflexes—all the things that our body does automatically, including emotions. Misophonia was clearly an emotional response, so I decided to apply my training to this new and mysterious condition. I love a challenge, and this was definitely a challenge. I love to help people, and this seemed like a worthwhile way to help my family and others.

I am also a very tenacious and determined person. When I set my mind to accomplish something, I stay focused and keep moving forward, despite surprises and roadblocks. Understanding misophonia has been an exciting challenge with many surprises and roadblocks. It has also been technically challenging developing methods to treat misophonia, including developing smartphone apps, but the opportunity to help others has been very rewarding. We have made great progress, but we still have much to do.

It is my hope that this book will help you understand misophonia. You are not crazy, and you were not just born this way. I hope this book will help you make immediate changes that can reduce the agony and emotional upheaval of misophonia, and that you will understand how you can start the process of overcoming this condition. It took years to develop all of your triggers, and it will take time to overcome them. I wish you well in your new journey to overcome your misophonia. So let's get started.

Misophonia is a condition where a person has an extreme emotional response to commonly occurring soft sounds or visual images. These are called "triggers" because they trigger the emotional response of anger and disgust. The anger may be any form such is irritation, anger, hatred, or rage. Triggers also demand your attention, and when they are happening, they prevent you from thinking about anything else. If you're reading this book because you think you have misophonia, you're probably thinking, "How can little noises have such an overpowering negative effect on me? How (and why) do such noises cause me to feel such irrational anger or disgust?"

If you're reading the book because someone close to you has misophonia, you have probably thought it inconceivable that the misophonic person has such an extreme response to something as harmless as the sound of a crunch from eating a chip or a sniffle. This just doesn't make sense. At least at some point, you probably thought, this is all in their head. This can't be real. But it is real—very real. And it is likely more horrible that you can imagine.

In this book, I'll present stories of real people with misophonia. Some are my patients, and others are those I have met along the way. Each gave their permission to have their story included because they want to help others understand this condition. I've changed their names for their privacy. Here are two typical stories from people just like you who hope to find relief from this debilitating condition.

Ryan's Story

"I've dealt with misophonia since I was a child. I think it started around the age of six or seven. My parents would raise their voices when reprimanding me and I would quickly cover my ears and beg them to stop yelling at me. They weren't even close to actually yelling at me, but on top of having this disorder, I also have above average hearing. I hear one pitch above and one pitch below the normal hearing range. This was medically proven by an ear, nose and throat doctor I went to because my mother talked through one of my hearing tests at the doctor so they thought I was half deaf.

"I find my triggers have continued to grow over the years. Chewing was really all that bothered me, but once I went to college my triggers grew at a staggering rate. I'm now triggered by any kind of chewing; even knowing someone is going to eat in the same room as me makes me get up and leave before they start eating because I have anxiety knowing what's about to happen. Birds chirping (this started during my freshmen year of college because birds chirped nonstop outside of our dorm room window), pens clicking, nails tapping, the text message clicking sound, heavy breathing, noise through the wall of any kind, but especially the bass in music or people's voices, sniffling, someone clearing their throat – the list goes on and on. Basically my misophonia has gotten to the point that any sound, if repetitive, will make me freak out. It's like I'm constantly alert and my ears are always searching for trigger sounds, which is why I sleep with headphones and white noise and a box fan on high every night.

"My friends and family have known something was up for so long that the second I hear a trigger sound I turn and look at them with this 'if you don't stop making that noise I will kill you' look, and they instantly stop what they're doing and apologize. Their apology after they've stopped making a trigger sound makes me feel bad because they shouldn't have to apologize for doing normal things like eating. Logically I know they shouldn't have to alter

3

their behavior because they're not doing it on purpose and the sounds that bother me are normal everyday sounds, but in the moment all I can think about is that sound, and if I can't remove myself – which I most often do – I will lose my mind and freak out. For example, I used to live at college and I could hear my neighbors through the wall of my room, and because I couldn't get away from it I flipped and started banging on the wall and screaming at the top of my lungs, all while shaking with anger and rage flowing through my veins. Afterwards I felt stupid for flipping out, but I couldn't help it, I couldn't get away from the sound, and after about five minutes it feels like people are making sounds to purposely piss me off. Needless to say my dorm director called me a handful and I no longer live at college.

"Since finding this website and showing the research to my family, they are much more understanding, my mother more than my father (his chewing is my biggest trigger in the entire world – even when he chews with his mouth closed – and he's constantly biting his nails or his lip or the skin inside his mouth). By the way, Tourette syndrome runs in my family, and my sister and father have it, so you can imagine how difficult it is to have misophonia and live with people who can't help but do things repetitively. Basically I've come to the point that I spend the majority of my time in my bedroom, alone. I don't mind being alone, and frankly I feel less on edge when I'm by myself because I know that I'm not going to hear a trigger sound. On the other side of that coin is the fact that I live with my family, but I rarely see them because I'm constantly in my room. Additionally, sudden loud sounds make me jump out of my skin, so at this point being deaf seems like the only way I would be able to spend time around other people.

"Does anyone know any tips or anything that may help me and decrease my isolation? Any advice is helpful because I love my family and I want to spend time with them, but I find it impossible to do so."

Bill's Story

"I feel like I know everyone else's story by heart and can relate to all. After a recent crisis and diagnosis, I've been examining this and other sites like it. Thank-you to all who have shared their stories. I've struggled with the symptoms of this condition for as long as I can remember. The first vivid memory I have is during a 2,600-mile-long family road trip where I noticed my younger brother was breathing loudly. I alerted my mother, who assured me he was OK. In a short time this had escalated into yelling, and me positioning my head against the window and my bicep in such a way that I couldn't hear him.

"This scene played out over and over in my family. Mealtimes were anxiety-provoking, and filled with anger, hurt feelings, abandonment and self-loathing. I rarely ate with my folks and brother at mealtime. I rarely accompanied them on family outings. Believing I liked nature, I remember searching for secluded places outdoors. I wonder now if I wasn't seeking some relief. University was hell—sniffles, gum chewing/popping, coughing, shuffling feet. Towards the end of my program I did not go to class but studied on my own or with a close friend. Miso has played a part in all my significant relationships, contributing to a divorce.

"I developed an addiction at an early age but have been sober for twenty-seven years (not always easy). It's hard for me to overlook how the possibility of using a substance to manage miso could be problematic. I'm fifty-one years old now and feel like I'm starting something new again. As I said earlier, this diagnosis puts my life in a new perspective. I had forgotten about the mealtime anxieties and self-loathing, the look on my brother's face when I'd look at him in rage and hatred. I hated myself for this; no one deserves those looks. I thought my mother hated me and regretted my birth. I can't ignore how difficult life with me must have been. In the end I became a loner, finding it easier to be alone than with others. There have been significant people in my life, but miso has always surfaced.

"The aspect of this diagnosis that I find hopeful is how it may just be legitimate. I say that with respect to all that believe its legitimacy. I've spent my whole life being told and believing 'it's all in my head' or 'just ignore it,' and believing that I was fundamentally broken. I'm in a relationship now with a reasonably understanding lady who says we can work this out. I hope we can, because I'm tired of believing I'm broken.

"I want to acknowledge how difficult it is for those around me and at the same time respect my struggles. I've never considered that maybe there is a possibility that this thing is beyond my control and that it is OK to ask for help. It sounds like a fairytale... thinking I can ask for help. I've got a lot of respect for all those who have put themselves on the line asking for help with this from those around them.

"Thanks for giving me this opportunity to express this."

Misophonia Triggers

For a person who suffers with misophonia, his or her personal *triggers* are a central fact of life. A trigger is a sound or sight that causes a misophonic response. It may be a sound someone makes when chewing, a slight pop of the lips when speaking, or a person whistling. For a person with misophonia, a trigger causes an involuntary reaction of irritation, and if the trigger continues, the emotions quickly become extreme anger, rage, hatred, or disgust. These emotions are jerked out of the person, and trying to stay calm when being triggered is futile.

The immediate negative emotions to a trigger are the hallmark of misophonia. Along with the emotions come physiological (bodily) actions that go along with such emotions. These include increased general muscle tension, increased heart rate, sweating, and feelings of overwhelming distress. When the trigger ceases, the emotional upheaval generally continues. Many people continue to hear the sound in their mind and replay the experience in their mind. While it may only take a few minutes for a person to become extremely distraught from the triggers, it can take hours for the person to calm down and resume normal life.

The impact of misophonia can vary from almost nothing to debilitating. I met a man who has only one trigger, and it's the sound of a spoon stirring a glass of iced tea. The tinkle sound is intolerable for him, but no one in his family drinks iced tea, so he rarely hears that trigger. His misophonia has little to no impact on his life. On the other hand, I met another person who also has only one trigger, and it is ruining her life. Her trigger is the sound of two or more women talking to each other. As a student in a mostly female discipline, she is subjected to this trigger continually at school, making her school experience hellacious.

Misdiagnoses

Many people with life-long misophonia have suffered because of being misdiagnosed. Traditionally, because virtually no one in the medical and psychological communities was aware of misophonia, any examination of an individual with misophonia resulted in a misdiagnosis. I asked members of an online misophonia support group to tell me their diagnoses prior to realizing they had misophonia. Here is a partial list: intermittent explosive disorder, oppositional defiant disorder, mood disorder, hyperacusis, ADD/ADHD, bipolar, paranoid personality disorder, obsessive compulsive disorder, anxiety, autism, nervous disorder, sensory processing disorder, phobia, typical mother-daughter issues, migraines, seizures, PTSD, and depression. Because any diagnosis without knowing about misophonia is a misdiagnosis, the best answer any professional can provide is, "I don't know."

Additionally, many people have been told that there was nothing wrong with them. They were told they just needed to get on with their lives, or that they were spoiled brats, crazy, too sensitive, a prima donna, never happy, stuck up, or hypersensitive.

Many were also told they needed to ignore the sounds or that it was all in their head. Misophonia causes extreme negative emotions and many individuals engage in inappropriate overt behavior (actions) directed against people they dearly love. Both the extreme emotions and actions cause high levels of guilt and shame, which is only made worse if the person is told it is their entire fault!

Here is a poem that expresses what it is like to have misophonia.

"My Misophonia"

By Angela Muriel Inez Mackay

My misophonia is not a quirk.
It's not what "makes her different"
It's not something fresh air can fix, or a pill can subside.

My misophonia is not intolerance.
It's not an excuse to be "bitchy,"
and it is most certainly NOT that time of the month.

These tears are not from sadness.
They are from anger, and being overwhelmed.
They're from the fear that it will be too much.
That it will push you away.

I do not wear headphones in defiance,
or in disrespect to your words.
I wear headphones for an ironic sense of quiet.

"It's not you, it's me" is my motto.
It's what I repeat in my head while you chew,
Each bite slicing into my ears like knives,
Each scrape of the fork a flinch of my finger,
Each crumple of the bag a cringe.

It kills me when you take joy in my pain,
Your gum mocks me,
And instead of an apology, you say,
"It's just a sound!"

To you, it IS just a sound.
But to me, it's my worst nightmare.

To me,
It's what makes me avoid people,
Avoid plans,
Avoid "grabbing a bite to eat" with friends.

It's what makes me want to stay home,
It's what makes me question why I even bother.

My misophonia is what fills me with fear
Every single day,
That I will be too much to handle,
That I'm too touchy,
That I'm too "intolerant",
My misophonia is part of me,
And I'm sorry.

I'm sorry for every glare,
Every cringe,
Every snappy word.

I'm sorry,
I have misophonia.

2. Diagnosing Misophonia

Misophonia is an extreme emotional reaction to typically occurring sounds. "Miso" means dislike or hatred, "phonia" means sounds, so "misophonia" means ''a dislike or hatred of sounds." This rather broad name was given to the disorder in 2001 by Drs. Pawel and Margaret Jastreboff.[1] I say "broad" because it's not about hating sounds in general; it's about hating only *specific* sounds. We call these *trigger sounds*. Additionally, the "hatred" of trigger sounds applies more to your involuntary response to a sound than your feelings about that sound.

This condition is also known as Selective Sound Sensitivity Syndrome, or 4S. This is the name given to this condition by audiologist Marsha Johnson, who first identified this condition in 1997.[2] This is really a better name for the condition because there are specific and selective sounds to which the person is extremely sensitive. However, misophonia is the more popular name for this condition now, and it also includes visual triggers.[3]

I have proposed that an even better name for this condition is Conditioned Aversive Reflex Disorder or CARD, which I will explain in a later chapter.

To define misophonia, let's first describe what misophonia is *not*.

Misophonia is not a sensitivity to the volume of the sound or to how loud the sound is. That's hyperacusis, and that's common, especially in small children. Hyperacusis can either develop in adulthood or continue from childhood. It can be tested by an audiologist by measuring the volume at which sound becomes painful. There are specific treatments that have been shown to reduce hyperacusis.

It's not a fear of a sound; that's phonophobia. And that's also common in children. Both hyperacusis and phonophobia are common with autism, for example, and in young children being scared by the toilet or the vacuum cleaner sound. This is not misophonia.

In children, Sensory Processing Disorder (SPD) can also cause an intolerance of loud sounds. SPD is a condition where a person has significant problems with multiple forms of sensory input such as touch, taste, smell, sight, and sounds. SPD is a general heightened sensitivity to sensory stimulation. It is not the same as misophonia, and it is not related to misophonia.[4] A child with SPD may appear to have hyperacusis or phonophobia because of the way he or she reacts to sounds.

Misophonia is not being irritated or upset by a continuous, loud, intrusive, or an irritating sound. There are people who, when they are in a situation where there's a repeating sound, become very upset. These people are generally considered a highly sensitive person (HSP). Their level of tolerance for these obnoxious or irritating situations is not as high as with most other people. And so they get upset. For example, a person living near an airport says that they have an extreme emotional reaction to the sound of airplanes flying over. This may or may not be misophonia. Misophonia is being upset (triggered) by a *single occurrence* of the trigger. Suppose they are not upset by the sound of a single airplane, but are upset by the first airplane in the morning, knowing that many more will follow. This is more likely to be a case of HSP than misophonia; they are upset because they know they will be hearing airplanes all day long. And the airplane noise is going to be intrusive and irritating. This person may be very, very, very distressed by the noise, and the extreme emotions may be identical to the emotions from misophonia. The level of distress does not determine whether a person does or does not have misophonia. The determining factor for misophonia is that a person triggers – has an immediate response of irritation or disgust – to a *single instance* of the trigger stimulus.

A person who is highly sensitive can also have misophonia. There may be certain sounds to which they are sensitive to because they are irritating sounds, but there are other sounds that are misophonic triggers.

Finally, misophonia is not reaction to a sound like nails on the chalkboard, a baby crying, a knife on a bottle, a disc grinder, or a female scream. It is common to be irritated by these sounds; . They are part of the top ten most irritating sounds. It seems that we are genetically wired to respond to these sounds because they are similar in frequency to a baby crying, a sound which should make us take action.

With misophonia there is an immediate reaction to the trigger stimulus. The trigger stimulus generally takes the form of sounds or sights, and the stimulus causes an immediate and involuntary response. It's a response that is jerked out of the person.

The triggers are generally soft sounds. If you don't have misophonia or if it's not a trigger sound you may not even hear the sound; but for a person with misophonia, if they are in a room and someone across the room starts doing something that is a trigger to them, such as popping their gum, they are going to hear it and feel it. This is common with a misophonia trigger.

There are also strong emotions with misophonia, the most universal being hate, anger, rage, disgust, resentment, and being offended. People with misophonia want to get away from the sound or make it stop, and in most cases are thinking of a verbal or a physical assault on the other person. Although it is extreme to think about physically hurting someone because of a sound they are making, rarely do people with misophonia act out on these impulses.

How to Determine if You Have Misophonia or Not

Suppose a person is triggered by a baby crying. This could be misophonia, but maybe not. The way to tell is to perform two tests. The general principle is that we need to rule out that the person is responding to the *volume* of the trigger or to the *meaning* of the trigger – in this case, a baby in distress. Both of these can be tested using a recorded trigger. First, test to see if the person is triggered by a low volume cry. The crying needs to be a real trigger with the volume reduced by distance or by playing the recorded crying at lower volumes. If the person is triggered regardless of volume, it is probably misophonia. Next see if the person is upset by the meaning of the trigger by making it obvious that you are using a recording. Because it is a recording, there is no baby in distress who needs to be helped, and the person knows the baby is not in distress. If the person is triggered to a soft sound (low volume crying) where the meaning (baby in distress) is not a factor, then the person has misophonia.

A person has misophonia if they have at least one trigger that creates the extreme emotional response in one setting. Of course, a clinical definition of misophonia will take into account the impact of the triggers on a person's life, but such a level has not been specified by the Diagnostic and Statistical Manual of Mental Disorders (DSM) which is used by psychologists and psychiatrists, or the International Statistical Classification of Diseases and Related Health Problems (ICD) which is used by health care providers.

Rating the Severity of Misophonia

There are three surveys I use to rate the severity of misophonia. These are the Misophonia Activation Scale, the Amsterdam Misophonia Scale, and the Misophonia Assessment Questionnaire. The Misophonia Activation Scale was developed by Misophonia-UK.org and is the simplest of the three.

Misophonia Activation Scale (MAS-1)

Please select the level that best describes what you experience.

Level 0: Person with misophonia hears a known trigger sound but feels no discomfort.

Level 1: Person with misophonia is aware of the presence of a known trigger person but feels no, or minimal, anticipatory anxiety.

Level 2: Known trigger sound elicits minimal psychic discomfort, irritation or annoyance. No symptoms of panic or fight or flight response.

Level 3: Person with misophonia feels increasing levels of psychic discomfort but does not engage in any physical response. Sufferer may be hyper-vigilant to audio-visual stimuli.

Level 4: Person with misophonia engages in a minimal physical response - non-confrontational coping behaviours, such as asking the trigger person to stop making the noise, discreetly covering one ear, or by calmly moving away from the noise. No panic or flight or flight symptoms exhibited.

Level 5: Person with misophonia adopts more confrontational coping mechanisms, such as overtly covering their ears, mimicking the trigger person, engaging in other echolalia, or displaying overt irritation.

Level 6: Person with misophonia experiences substantial psychic discomfort. Symptoms of panic, and a fight or flight response, begin to engage.

Level 7: Person with misophonia experiences substantial psychic discomfort. Increasing use (louder, more frequent) use of confrontational coping mechanisms. There may be unwanted sexual arousal. Sufferer may re-imagine the trigger sound and visual cues over and over again, sometimes for weeks, months or even years after the event.

Level 8: Person with misophonia experiences substantial psychic discomfort. Some violence ideation.

Level 9: Panic/rage reaction in full swing. Conscious decision not to use violence on trigger person. Actual flight from vicinity of noise and/or use of physical violence on an inanimate object. Panic, anger or severe irritation may be manifest in sufferer's demeanour.

Level 10: Actual use of physical violence on a person or animal (i.e., a household pet). Violence may be inflicted on self (self-harming).

Unwanted sexual arousal can occur with an intense misophonic response, as listed at level seven, but only one of my patients has ever mentioned this. I had several patients who reported an unpleasant sexual arousal reflex occurring at all levels of misophonia severity. This is explained later, but for now, I suggest you do not consider sexual arousal as a primary factor in determining your misophonia severity. Virtually everyone with misophonia has wide variation in their response to triggers based on the situation, the trigger, and how long it continues. I suggest you rate yourself at the highest level you experience in a typical week.

Amsterdam Misophonia Scale (A-MISO-S)

The Amsterdam Misophonia Scale (A-MISO-S) is an adaptation of the Yale-Brown Obsessive-Compulsive Scale (Y-BOCS) and was developed by researchers in Amsterdam.[5] The severity of your misophonia is determined by the sum of the points from these questions.

AMSTERDAM MISOPHONIA SCALE: Rate the characteristics of each item during the prior week up until and including the time you fill out this survey. Scores should reflect the average (mean) occurrence of each item for the entire week.

Q1. How much of your time is occupied by misophonic triggers? How frequently do the (thoughts about the) misophonic triggers occur?

0: None

1: Mild - less than 1 hr/day, or occasionally (thoughts about) triggers (no more than 5 times a day)

2: Moderate - 1 to 3 hrs/day, or frequent (thoughts about) triggers (no more than 8 times a day, most of the hours are unaffected).

3: Severe - greater than 3 hrs and up to 8 hrs/day or very frequent (thoughts about) triggers.

4: Extreme - greater than 8 hrs/day or near constant (thoughts about) triggers.

Q2. How much do these misophonic triggers interfere with your social, work or role functioning? (Is there anything that you don't do because of them? If currently not working, determine how much performance would be affected if you were employed.)

0: None

1: Mild - slight interference with social or occupational/school activities, but overall performance not impaired.

2: Moderate - definite interference with social or occupational performance, but still manageable.

3: Severe - causes substantial impairment in social or occupational performance.

4: Extreme - incapacitating.

Q3. How much distress do the misophonic triggers cause you? (In most cases, distress is equated with irritation, anger, or disgust. Only rate the emotion that seems triggered by misophonic triggers, not generalized irritation or irritation associated with other conditions.)

0: None

1: Mild - occasional irritation/distress.

2: Moderate - disturbing irritation/anger/disgust, but still manageable.

3: Severe - very disturbing irritation/anger/disgust.

4: Extreme - near constant and disturbing anger/disgust.

Q4. How much effort do you make to resist the (thoughts about the) misophonic triggers? (How often do you try to disregard or turn your attention away from these triggers? Only rate effort made to resist, not success or failure in actually controlling the thought or sound.)

0: Makes an effort to always resist, or symptoms so minimal, doesn't need to actively resist.

1: Tries to resist most of the time.

2: Makes some effort to resist.

3: Yields to all (thoughts about) misophonic triggers without attempting to control them, but does so with some reluctance.

4: Completely and willing yields to all obsessions.

Q5. How much control do you have over your thoughts about the misophonic triggers? How successful are you in stopping or diverting your thinking about the misophonic triggers? Can you dismiss them?

0: Complete control.

1: Much control - usually able to stop or divert thoughts about misophonic triggers.

2: Moderate control - sometimes able to stop or divert thoughts about misophonic triggers.

3: Little control - rarely successful in stopping or dismissing thoughts about misophonic triggers, can only divert attention with difficulty.

4: No control - experience thoughts as completely involuntary, rarely able to alter thinking about misophonic triggers.

Q6. Have you been avoiding doing anything, going any place, or being with anyone because of your misophonia? (How much do you avoid, for example, by using other loud sounds, such as music?)

0: No deliberate avoidance.

1: Mild, minimal avoidance. Less than an hr/day or occasional avoidance.

2: Moderate, some avoidance. 1 to 3 hr/day or frequent avoidance.

3: Severe, much avoidance. Greater than 3 up to 8 hr/day. Very frequent avoidance.

4: Extreme very extensive avoidance. Greater than 8 hr/day. Doing almost everything you can to avoid triggering symptoms.

Finally:

What would be the worst thing that could happen to you if you were not able to avoid the misophonic triggers?

Describe:

_____

The sum score of these questions determines the severity rating as follows:

– 0-4: Subclinical (meaning you do not need treatment)
– 5-9: Mild
– 10-14: Moderate
– 15-19: Severe
– 20-24: Extreme

Misophonia Assessment Questionnaire

Marsha Johnson developed a survey for use with her patients. It's called the Misophonia Assessment Questionnaire. The survey consists of 21 questions that are scored from 0 to 3 points based on how often the item applies to you. The severity of your misophonia is determined by the sum of the points from these questions.

MISOPHONIA ASSESSMENT QUESTIONNAIRE	
RATING SCALE: 0 = not at all, 1 = a little of the time, 2 = a good deal of the time, 3 = almost all the time	Score
1. My sound issues currently make me unhappy	
2. My sound issues currently create problems for me.	
3. My sound issues have recently made me feel angry.	
4. I feel that no one understands my problems with certain sounds.	
5. My sound issues do not seem to have a known cause.	
6. My sound issues currently make me feel helpless.	

7. My sound issues currently interfere with my social life.	
8. My sound issues currently make me feel isolated.	
9. My sound issues have recently created problems for me in groups.	
10. My sound issues negatively affect my work/school life (currently or recently).	
11. My sound issues currently make me feel frustrated.	
12. My sound issues currently impact my entire life negatively.	
13. My sound issues have recently made me feel guilty.	
14. My sound issues are classified as "crazy."	
15. I feel that no one can help me with my sound issues.	
16. My sound issues currently make me feel hopeless.	
17. I feel that my sound issues will only get worse with time.	
18. My sound issues currently impact my family relationships.	
19. My sound issues have recently affected my ability to be with other people.	
20. My sound issues have not been recognized as legitimate.	
21. I am worried that my whole life will be affected by sound issues.	
Sum Score	

Dr. Johnson divided the scale into thirds. The lower third (0-21) is mild. The middle third (22-42) is moderate, and the upper third (43-63) is severe.[6] You can take this survey and rate your misophonia. It would seem to make more sense to divide the scale into five zones, as with the A-MISO-S survey. With five zones, the ratings would be

– 0-11: Subclinical (meaning you do not need treatment)
– 12-24: Mild
– 25-37: Moderate
– 38-50: Severe
– 51-63: Extreme

These assessments can be a valuable way to track the progress of your misophonia over time. Because change in misophonia symptoms is often slow (whether increasing or decreasing in severity) and treatment programs can take six months or more, it can be beneficial to fill out these forms regularly to track your progress when you are engaged in a treatment program.

3. Triggers, Triggers, and More Triggers

Misophonia triggers generally start with a familiar person and a familiar sound:. it's something in the person's life. I conducted a survey of individuals with misophonia in 2013 in which two-thirds said their worst trigger was an eating/chewing sound, and 10% were breathing sounds. The remaining 25% had a variety of "worst triggers" including bass through walls, a dog barking, coughing, clicking sounds, whistling, parents talking, sibilance (the sound produced when saying words such as *sun* or *chip*), and someone typing on a keyboard. This is by no means a complete list of triggers. In fact, it is virtually impossible to make a complete list because a trigger can be virtually any repeating sound or sight. Although much less common, triggers can also be touch, smell, and vibrations.

Triggers are sounds we hear in everyday life. Eating sounds and dinner table sounds are very common in our lives, and are the most common triggers for misophonia. The second most common triggers are breathing or nose sounds, such as nose whistles, heavy breathing, sighing, snoring, and anything associated with breathing. But really, a trigger can be any repeating sound. And the list of known triggers is like the list of all repeating sounds in the world.

It's not that these sounds become triggers because of the sound itself. They become triggers because the person hears the sound in a specific situation and they develop a misophonic response to that sound.

As mentioned, we find that triggers start with one sound or one person making a particular noise, and then the trigger spreads to similar sounds, other places, anyone making the already offensive sound, and sights associated with those sounds. So with time these triggers spread and spread. We will cover this in detail in the chapter on Developing New Triggers.

Misophonia can start with a visual trigger, but this is very rare. In fact, I have seen only one report of misophonia starting with a visual trigger. Generally it starts with an auditory trigger, and then visual images that occur immediately before the trigger can become a visual trigger. For example, if I trigger to chewing, then seeing someone put food into their mouth could become a trigger. I could also develop a trigger to seeing someone bring food toward their mouth or to pick up a potato chip.

Images that occur with the trigger can also become trigger stimuli. For example, jaw movement associated with chewing is very commonly reported as a visual trigger by someone who triggers to gum popping.

Visual triggers can even be images that occur repeatedly *after* being triggered, although this is less common. Also, we find that repetitive movements such as leg jiggling or hair twirling are common trigger stimuli, but it's not clear why. I had a patient suggest it was because it was a nervous behavior.

Common Misophonic Triggers
Sound (Auditory) Triggers:
- Sounds of people eating – all forms of chewing, crunching, smacking, swallowing, talking with food mouth
- Sounds made at the table – fork on plate, fork scraping teeth, spoon on bowl, clinking of glasses
- Sounds of people drinking – sipping, slurping, saying "ah" after a drink, swallowing, breathing after a drink
- Other mouth sounds – sucking teeth, lip popping, kissing, flossing, brushing teeth
- Associated sounds – opening chip bags, water bottle crinkling, setting a cup down
- Breathing sounds – sniffing, snorting, nasally breathing, regular breathing, snoring, nose whistle, yawing, coughing, throat clearing, hiccups

- Vocal triggers – consonant sounds (S and P especially), vowel sounds (less common), lip pop, dry mouth voice, gravelly voice, whispering, specific words, muffled talking, several people talking at once, TV through walls, singing, humming, whistling, "uh"
- Home sounds – bass through walls, door slamming, refrigerator running, hair dryers, electric shavers, nail clipping, foot shuffling, lip flops, heavy footsteps, walking of people upstairs, joint cracking, scratching, ticking clocks, pipes knocking, baby crying, toilet flushing
- Work/school sounds – typing, mouse clicks, page flipping, pencil on paper, copier sound, pen clicking, pen tapping, tapping on desk
- Other - Farm equipment, pumps, lawnmowers, bouncing balls, back-up beepers, traffic noise, beep of car locking, car door slamming
- Animal sounds – dogs/cat grooming, dogs barking, rooster crowing, birds singing, crickets, frogs, animal scratching, dog whimpering

Sight (Visual) Triggers – Jaw movement chewing, hand touching face, scrolling on smartphone, pointing, leg jiggling, hair twirling, putting food into mouth, drumming fingers, blinking eyes

Odor (Olfactory) Triggers – certain scents (rare)

Touch (Tactile) Triggers – touching a keyboard, touching certain fabrics (rare)

Other Triggers – vibration from anything such as bass, bumping desk, kicking chair, heavy footsteps

4. Oh, the Emotions!

An extreme emotional response is the trademark of misophonia. Here is a comment someone with misophonia posted on misophoniatreatment.com.

Judy's Story

"I have only recently found out that there was a name for my condition. I am fifty-four years old have suffered what seems like forever with this problem. One particular person at work drives me crazy sniffing and coughing all the time. At times I get so I angry I think I could kill. I even get to the point of wishing this person would drop dead (bad I know), but I'm sure other sufferers feel the same at times. My poor lovely husband knows how I feel and tries his best not to make the noises I detest. I sometimes don't know how he lives with me. I know I have passed this on to one of my girls, and my dad had it, too. It's making my social life a nightmare."

Note that she wishes the person making the noise would drop dead! It is hard for someone who does not have misophonia to understand the extent of emotions that are caused by being repeatedly triggered, especially in a situation where the misophonic individual is trapped and cannot make the triggers stop.

Below is a twenty-six-question survey of emotional responses to triggers. I use this survey for my new misophonia patients. As you read through these, you will see that the list of emotions/reactions go from mild to extreme. All of these emotions are often rated as "none of the time," "a little of the time," "a good deal of the time," or "almost all the time."

Misophonia Emotional Responses

0) None of the time, 1) A little of the time, 2) A good deal of the time, 3) Almost all of the time

1. You hear a known trigger sound. You may dislike the sound.
2. You hear a trigger sound and feel annoyed or upset.
3. You want the other person to know how upset you are.
4. You want the person to stop making the sound.
5. You want to force the other person to stop making the sound.
6. You feel you must see that the person is actually making the sound or doing what you think they are doing. You want to keep looking or stare.
7. You want to hear something else, so you don't hear the sound.
8. You want to be physically far away from the sound.
9. You wish you were deaf.
10 You are afraid that if you do something, you will hurt others' feelings.
11. You want to get away from the sound, but do not want to make a scene.
12. You want to get away from the sound as quickly as possible, even if it would be embarrassing.
13. You want to push, poke, shove, etc., the person making the sound.
14. You want to verbally assault of the person making the noise.
15. You want to physically assault the person making the noise.
16. You want to physically hurt or harm the other person.
17. You want to scream or cry loudly.
18. You feel anger.
19. You feel rage.
20. You hate the person.
21. You feel disgust.
22. You feel resentment.
23. You feel you need to escape, flee, or run away.
24. You want to get revenge.
25. You feel offended by the person making the noise.
26. You feel despair or hopeless.

One person may respond with "not at all" to a few of these questions, but most people with misophonia experience over 75%

of the feelings expressed on this list. In general, individuals will have all of these emotions except for two or three, which are unique to each individual. Misophonia causes extreme emotions in virtually everyone.

5. Oh, the Guilt!

Generally those suffering with misophonia feel guilty about the way they think and act when being triggered. We typically reserve the list of powerful emotions discussed in the previous chapter for our worst enemies or times when we're greatly offended, but people with misophonia regularly direct these response to those who are closest to them. The ugly miso-emotions are literally jerked out of the misophonic individual when they are being triggered. Additionally, once the fight-or-flight response kicks in, the person may scream, verbally assault, or even push, poke, and shove the person who caused the trigger. If looks could kill, everyone around the misophonic person would be dead!

Nearly everyone with misophonia feels a varying degree of guilt after being triggered. Most feel a great deal of guilt because they recognize that their response was out of proportion to what the triggering person did. For example, children are often triggered by a parent. One person reported that their trigger person was their stepfather, whom they dearly loved.. He was a great man, even his hero. But when riding in the car, the stepdad would chew gum and suddenly the child experienced nearly every emotion affiliated with misophonia, including wanting to hurt his stepdad. Afterwards, he person felt guilty for wanting to hurt someone, especially someone he loved so dearly.

Guilt is also very common for a parent who has a child that triggers them. The love of the parent for the child is inconsistent with the rage felt toward that child for making an innocuous sound like sniffling. Again, guilt follows.

Misophonia generally develops to sounds made by someone who spends a lot of time with the misophonic individual. Except in cases where there is an embroiled relationship, that is full of conflict, abuse, and contention, the strong miso-emotions are directed toward a loved one, and are inconsistent with the emotional bond with that person. Guilt is common when we act differently than we think we should act, which is why it is such a recurring emotion among misophonics.

If you have misophonia, have empathy for yourself. Guilt is the feeling a person has when they have intentionally done something wrong. If a child steals candy from the store, then they should feel guilty for doing that. If a sales clerk accidentally gives you five dollars extra in change and you know it, you should feel guilty for keeping the money because you chose to do something that was not honest. But if you get the extra change, only to discover it later, you should not feel guilty because you did not do choose to do something that violates your moral values.

If you have misophonia, you may have horrible feelings toward a loved one; but you are not *choosing* to have these feelings. These feelings are literally yanked out of you, or imposed on you by your misophonia. They are not really "your" feelings or feelings you have decided to express toward that person. They are an emotional reflex. As previously discussed, a reflex is an involuntary response to a stimulus. In this case, the emotions simply happen as a direct result of being triggered.

Because you are not choosing to have horrible feelings toward a person you love, try replacing your guilt with regret. You don't want to have such ill feelings about someone after they trigger you, and you regret that you have them. If you want to be tall, but your height is only five feet, then you can regret that you are not taller; but because it is not your choice, guilt is an inappropriate emotion. So be good to yourself. Beating yourself up and feeling guilty about your miso-emotions doesn't help in any way. Anything that decreases your feeling of wellbeing will increase your misophonia. So smile, and realize that at this stage, the extreme miso-emotions are beyond your control.

However, there is hope! You do have a degree of control over how you respond when you have misophonia triggers. These are your coping behaviors. If your coping behaviors (fifth box on the drawing below) are aggressive, then you can and should work to change those.

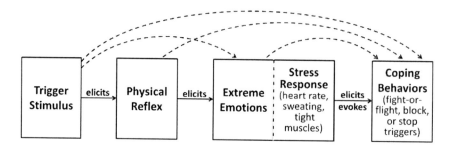

Although difficult, you can (and should) manage them by deciding what you want to do when you are triggered. One of the easiest ways of reducing aggressive coping behaviors is to reduce the number of triggers you experience, especially situations where you cannot escape the triggers. I know it sounds like a lot for now, but relax: we will talk more about how to do this in the chapter on misophonia management techniques. For now, I just want you to stop beating yourself up over the things you've felt and said as a result of your misophonia, and instead take the time to regret some of your misophonia-induced feelings and behaviors.

6. Prevalence of Misophonia

How common is misophonia? Many consider it a rare disease, and on rare disease day (the last day of February), many on the Facebook misophonia group express a desire to speak out about misophonia. In the United States, a rare disease has officially been defined as one that affects less than 200,000 people in the US, which is about one in 1,500 people (0.07%). By this definition misophonia is not a rare disease. It is a "rarely known" disorder.

I did my first survey on misophonia in February of 2013 on different characteristics of individuals with misophonia. I was trying to determine how misophonia develops and if there were certain characteristics people with misophonia have in common. I wanted to have a control group to compare some of the personality traits and characteristics, and so I sent the survey to my LinkedIn contacts. Much to my surprise, 5% of my LinkedIn contacts had misophonic reactions. And so I thought, wow, this is not some extremely unusual phenomenon here. In fact, I had people with misophonia popping up all over the place.

I paid for a survey using SurveyMonkey.com, where they randomly solicited individuals who had no connection to misophonia. These were just individuals who were willing to fill out surveys to have fifty cents donated to the cause of their choice. I purchased three hundred and I got ten extra for free. I made sure that the title of the survey did not mention sound or sensitivities. I gave the same survey to a group of people with misophonia to determine a standard of reference for my SurveyMonkey group. Out of the 310 people surveyed (50% of them women, 50% men), I found that 15.2% had reactions suggesting misophonia. It was more common among the women (18.6%) than it was among of the men (11.6%).[7] Rather than being a *rare* disease, which is one in 1,500, it was a *rarely known* but common disorder with about 225 in 1,500 having misophonia.

That was actually a higher number that I expected. I was expecting 5% to 10%, but it came in at 15%. In 2014, there was an official published peer reviewed study that came out of the University of South Florida's College of Medicine and their psychology department. They used undergraduate psychology students. (This is very common in college research; they give psychology students a little extra credit for taking a survey or participating in some form of research for the graduate students.) They had almost 500 participants in this study, and 84% were women, so that would tend to raise the percentage of incidence of misophonia. Their study was comprehensive enough to see how the misophonia affected the individual's life. What they found was that 20% had clinically significant misophonia,[8] significant meaning they had to alter their life in some regard in order to handle their triggers. This finding surprised me since 20% is higher than what I had previously observed.

However, since 84% of the participants were female, the finding that 20% had misophonia is very similar to my survey that found 18.6% of women had misophonia triggers.

A recent blog post on the family ancestry website 23andMe.com mentioned an internal study conducted with about 80,000 customers, in which people were asked "Does the sound of other people chewing fill you with rage? (Yes/No/Not Sure)." About 20% replied yes. They also found that the affirmative response was more common in women.[9] Unfortunately they only reported the *yes* and *no* numbers, and excluded the *not sure*. I am concerned that those who were *not sure* probably don't have misophonia so the prevalence of misophonia is lower than their reported number, but at least it provides general support for the prevalence of misophonia of the other two studies.

The takeaway from this is that misophonia is really quite common – perhaps affecting approximately 15% of adults. It is more common in women than in men, but many, many people suffer in silence, or they are written off as being grouchy, cranky, or irritable. If this number is correct, which research is beginning to confirm it is, there could be forty million people with misophonia in the United States alone.

Considering these statistics and the fact that misophonia is not widely studied, if you randomly selected a doctor or therapist and then another individual, it is more likely that the random individual would *have* misophonia than the doctor or therapist would *know about* misophonia.

7. Diversity of Misophonia

Many people consider misophonia a condition that is the same for everyone where everyone has the same symptoms. It is true that there is a group of common triggers (such as eating sounds) and common emotional reactions (anger, hatred, rage, and disgust). It often starts during the late childhood years (six to twelve) and becomes much worse in the teen years. But within this apparently uniform condition there is much variation.

What are the differences from person to person that we see? We can identify diversity in four areas:

1. The age of onset.
2. When it becomes severe.
3. Trigger sounds.
4. Initial physical reflexes.

The Age of Onset

I conducted a survey of 200 people with misophonia in March of 2013 of 200. Seventy-five percent of those completing the survey were women. The most common age for misophonia to begin was nine to ten years. Twenty-five percent had their misophonia begin at this age. Twenty-one percent had their misophonia begin at age seven to eight, and 20% began at age eleven or twelve years. This seems to demonstrate that misophonia begins at a typical age, but the survey also showed that there is a wide variation in the age of onset. In that survey people started having misophonia from as young as age four to as old as age fifty-five. It became severe from age four all the way up to sixty-four. So there was really a wide range in the age when misophonia begins.

In the graph below, the dark bars show the ages when people started having misophonia, and the light bars are when their misophonia became severe. Although we have a clear majority of the people whose misophonia begins at ages seven to twelve years, and became severe from age seven to sixteen, about half of the people fell outside of these ages. If misophonia was a purely hereditary condition like puberty, you would find that the age of onset and severity would be more uniform. Also, you would not see a range in age from four to fifty-five years for onset. You don't find people going into puberty at age thirty, but with misophonia we find a scattering of ages for the start of misophonia.

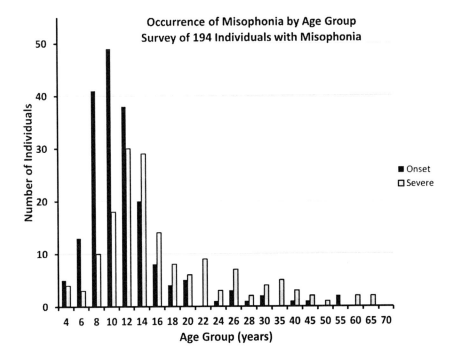

We also find there's quite a diversity of triggers. Although there are common triggers such as mouth and breathing sounds, the list of triggers comprises almost every repeating noise. No one has all of these triggers; everyone has their own set of triggers. So even though there are many common trigger sounds, there is a lot of variation in the sounds from person to person.

The first trigger that you get is specific to a single person or thing that is part of the individual's life in some way. It depends on the sounds you are hearing. There are also particular sounds such as bird chirps, crickets, pipes knocking, things that people say, oxygen system noise, and many more. There are general triggers that will affect many people – popcorn, loud eating, gum popping (which seems to be a very common trigger), but you may also have triggers that are caused by a single person, at least that's where they start.

Some people are triggered only when a certain individual makes a specific sound. For example, I was working with a fifteen-year-old young man who triggered to the sound of his mom eating crunchy food. We had him face the wall. I popped a Frito in my mouth. I crunched it. No response, nothing. His mom put a Frito in her mouth and crunched it, and he said, "Ugh! That's it." For another person, it didn't matter who made the sound. Any crunch triggered him.

I worked with a person whose trigger was their husband saying, "uh." This monosyllabic utterance didn't trigger anyone else, and other people could make the same sound without it affecting her. It was her unique trigger. Another person triggered when her husband ate crunchy bread. We know of kids who trigger to a parent's voice, but not to other voices. I know a man who started triggering in midlife when some birds built their nest outside of his window. It seems like that would not be a big deal, but it was his bedroom window and they were mockingbirds, which sing twenty-four hours a day. He developed misophonia to those specific bird chirps.

Non-human sounds such as pipes knocking, clocks ticking, hair dryers, electric shavers, and such are also triggers for some, but not triggers for most people. Everybody has their own unique set of triggers. So although there's commonality, there's still uniqueness, and these particular triggers are based on your individual experience, the ones that you have heard, and are not based on an automatic biological time clock. It is based on your unique experiences with those sounds.

It seems we have many common triggers because we have fairly common experiences, such as eating together or being close enough to hear another person breathe. It is customary to eat together, during which time we hear others eating, and so many people develop triggers to eating sounds. If you have someone in your home with allergies, you hear lots of nasally breathing, so we have lots of people who develop triggers to breathing sounds. Since we have common life experiences, we develop some similar triggers, but also unique triggers.

The Individual Physical Reflex

A trigger produces an involuntary response or reflex. Ninety-five percent of the people I work with can identify a specific physical reflex to a trigger. They hear the sound and have a particular physical reflex. It may be the contraction of muscles in the neck, shoulders, chest, arms, face, hands open, hands closed, feet, legs, toes, or butt. It can be internal reflexes such as esophageal, intestinal, or stomach constriction, nausea, sexual arousal, or the urge to urinate. There's a wide range of reflexes. Sometimes the reflexes are complex and involve many muscles, such as a reflex feels like a ball is hitting your chest. This was the trigger reflex for one person. The uniqueness in the physical reflex of each individual is part of what suggests that misophonia is not just a genetic condition that kicks in, but is something that develops because of both the neurology and the experience of the person.

Some physical reflexes are almost imperceptible, such as a slight head jerk or a twitch of the eye. Others are very strong. One person described how hers felt as having a shovel stabbed through her chest and out her back. Another person said her reflex felt like someone was pulling a string out of her spine.. While there's going to be some repetition among thirty to forty million people who have misophonia triggers, these are unique physical responses and very few others would describe them in the same way.

The reflex can be difficult to perceive because of the strong emotions that you have. The overwhelming emotions that come immediately after the trigger can make it difficult to perceive that there was a physical reflex response. It is kind of a one-two punch – the little physical reflex and then these strong emotions, or the little physical reflex and then the fight-or-flight response. This makes the physical reflex hard to notice.

If you want to know your physical reflex, you need a very small trigger – short and quiet, maybe a half second or less, barely audible. You can record the sound of your trigger and then play it back so that you can adjust the volume. You can use a voice memo app on your phone, although that app will not allow you to control the length of the trigger. You can use the Misophonia Trigger Tamer app or the Misophonia Reflex Finder app, both of which I developed, to record the trigger and then control both the volume and the duration of the trigger. Some people need to have a session on the Neural Repatterning Technique, which I also developed. This treatment method, which uses the Trigger Tamer app, plays the very small trigger every thirty seconds or so, along with relaxing music. The trigger is so weak that you do not experience the negative misophonic emotions. You can recognize the reflex because you are relaxed and experience the trigger many times during a thirty-minute treatment.

8. Prognosis for Misophonia

If a person has misophonia, what's the prognosis?

I will provide hope later in the book, but first let me provide you with an overall view of misophonia. For one thing, misophonia doesn't just go away with time or getting older. Generally the severity of misophonia remains the same or gets progressively worse[10]. It can be stable for years and then escalate. Then remain at that elevated state for years and then escalate even more. It does seem to lessen at certain times. The upheaval associated with misophonia tends to lessen as the teen matures into adulthood, because they learn that they are going to be triggered and there's no other choice. They are just going to have to deal with this unpleasant reaction, and many people learn to suffer in silence. A child may scream and yell at her mom, but it doesn't get any better. She may scream and yell at her friends and be ostracized. Eventually the child learns that acting out only makes it worse and that she must cope. She learns to suffer in silence. One lady said that when she was triggered too much, she would just go into another room and cry. And people also learn to modify their life to cope with misophonia.

Many people with misophonia would never go to a movie theater because the popcorn crunching is there and they would find it intolerable. They also modify their work conditions. I know of one case where a person couldn't handle the trigger sounds in the classroom so he dropped out of M.I.T and became a machinist. Although the classroom noises triggered him, the sounds in the machinery created a trigger-free environment for him.

Unfortunately, we find that misophonia can be very detrimental to relationships. It really takes a caring, patient person to deal with a spouse who is triggered by the sounds they make.

Another situation that heightens misophonia is that triggers develop with prolonged experience with a particular person. A spouse or significant other may not trigger you at first, but with time, triggers develop. The same thing happens with children. It would be most unusual for your baby to trigger you, no matter how loud they ate. But with time, those cute little eating and breathing sounds change into the lip smacking and sniffling of an elementary school kid, and can become full strength triggers. We will talk about how to reduce the risk of developing new triggers in a later chapter.

9. Perception Versus Reality

We are going to use several simple figures in this chapter to show how you react to misophonic triggers. So let's start with a simple one about how it feels when you are triggered.

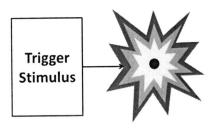

You hear or see a trigger, and ka-boom, there is an explosion. You feel extreme emotions that may include anger, disgust, rage, resentment, or that you're offended or being attacked. Some people have extreme feelings of helplessness or hopelessness. While all of these feelings are valid, let's take a more objective view of this misophonic response to triggers.

Involuntary Emotional Response

The misophonic response is an involuntary reaction that's jerked out of the person. They are not choosing to react. If we look at the brain in the figure below, there are three regions identified. Let's consider what is happening in each region.

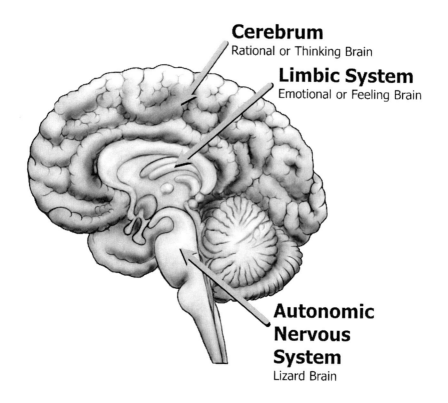

Cerebrum
Rational or Thinking Brain

Limbic System
Emotional or Feeling Brain

Autonomic Nervous System
Lizard Brain

At the top is the cerebrum, which is the thinking brain. With your thinking brain, you can think, "Okay, I'm going to stay calm." But with misophonia, the person can't stay calm when they are triggered.

The part at the bottom of our brain, in the brain stem, is called the autonomic nervous system. Many people call it the lizard brain. The lizard brain controls our reflexes, and this is the heart of misophonia.

The limbic system is what lights up when we have these strong emotions. Misophonia is a combination between the reflex reaction of the lizard brain and the emotional reaction of the limbic system that's just yanked out of the person. People with misophonia just can't stay calm when they are being triggered.

The popular view of this misophonic response or reflex is that you hear or see a trigger, and you immediately experience extreme emotions without intentionally doing so. This reaction is involuntary. You didn't have it at birth, so one would conclude that it's acquired, meaning you've developed it or it's developed. So now you hear this trigger and instantly feel the emotions. This is the popular view of misophonia as shown in the figure.

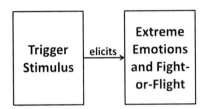

This is also the way that misophonia is described in peer reviewed journal articles, which report misophonia research studies..[11] In fact, there is one article entitled, "Misophonia: A Disorder of Emotion Processing of Sounds." But I find that misophonia is fundamentally not about the *emotional processing* of sounds. It is about a *physical sensation* that happens when you hear a trigger. You hear normal sounds, but you literally feel (physically) a trigger.

I've been told that a trigger is more like being slapped or being poked in the ribs with a stick or being zapped with a cattle prod or mini-Taser. I sometimes demonstrate to a non-misophonic person what a trigger is like by taking a rubber band, putting it against my chest, pulling back the center, and popping myself. Ouch! That hurts. That's the way I think of misophonia. It is an initial *"POW"* response. And it has very extreme emotions that come with the *"POW."*

There's quite a bit of diversity in this physical reflex. In my practice, I estimated that about 95% of those I had worked with had a physical reflex. However, I had four clear cases where no matter how hard we tried to identify a physical reflex, the only experience of the person to a trigger was an emotional response of irritation. I worked with one person a second time, and using a different test method, he felt a muscle jerk in his legs. After working with another person for over six months, one session she declared that she had identified her physical reflex. She said a coworker had asked her why she was mad, but she replied she was not. The coworker said, "Then why are you frowning? You frown almost all the time." My patient recognized that she did frown a lot, and that the frown was caused by her triggers. Every time she was triggered, her forehead muscles jerked, which are one of two sets of muscles involved in frowning. (the average Joe won't know what you shared in the comment and won't make the connection) That was her reflex. The third person reported not having a physical reflex, but the physical reflex in his face was visible. So with the people that I have worked with, about 99% have a physical reflex.

A lot people with misophonia say, "I simply have rage. I don't have a physical reflex," but when we get into a treatment setting or we get calm and do a test with a weak trigger, then they can identify the reflex. I worked with one girl who said she only had rage (no physical reflex at all). Yet whenever we used a very, very small trigger during treatment, you could see her shoulders jerk. She identified the muscle jerk herself when we finished the treatment and we talked about it. Incidentally, she did not feel the negative emotion during the treatment. She felt the muscle jerk reflex. This is shown in the figure below – that the misophonic trigger elicits the physical reflex, as shown in the next figure. (Note: Elicit is a technical term that means to "cause a reflex to happen.")

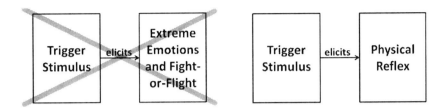

Now it's time to add the emotional response to your misophonic reflex response into our drawing. It appears that the emotional response is jerked out of you (elicited) by the sensation of the physical reflex as shown in the next figure.

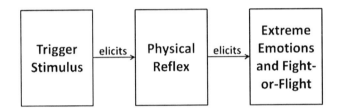

As noted above, misophonic individuals all reported that it was impossible for them to not become upset when exposed to trigger stimuli, although they had repeatedly tried to remain calm. It is commonly said that "anger is a choice," or that "another person cannot make you mad." This may be true for verbal behavior because the meaning of the words is determined by a person's learning experience with language and other social factors. A person's response to a statement such as "I hate you" is affected by their evaluation of the context and social dynamics at that moment.

With misophonia, however, anger is not a choice. There are two plausible constructs for emotional response being elicited by the initial physical reflex. The first construct is as follows. The sound elicits an intrusive, uncomfortable reflex response. I propose that this physical reflex response is a form of physical assault on the person, although the actual physical assault is performed by their autonomic nervous system. The response to the repetitive physical reflex is the array of the extreme emotions as shown above.

How about the emotional response? Well, you can't feel electricity, but if you've been shocked you felt something. What you felt was muscle contraction. The electricity made you tighten your muscles, and that was uncomfortable. We know that the reason our muscles move is that our brain sends out electrical impulses, which cause our muscles to constrict. So when the lizard brain perceives the trigger, it sends out an electrical shock! The emotional response to aversive events is consistent with research. The electric shock is an assault on your body, and it's that physical assault that produces the strong emotions.

Research studies have shown that aversive stimuli cause fight-or-flight emotions in humans.[12] The strength of these emotions is affected by a number of factors, and the urge to fight may not be visible through outward behavior. This is consistent with the emotions for misophonics, and the reported effort of misophonics to resist aggressive impulses. Furthermore, activity in the limbic system of humans in response to aversive odors and tastes has been demonstrated.[13] Evidence suggests that the aversive physical misophonic reflex may cause the commonly reported emotions of hate, anger, rage and disgust.

As I mentioned earlier, one woman reported feeling like a shovel was run through her sternum and out her back when she was being triggered, but said this was metaphorical, incorporating both the physical and emotional feelings. She couldn't describe which muscle was contracting, but she sure felt it. Her reflex was a gasp for breath. Do a quick exercise to gain an understanding of what that felt like for her. Close off your windpipe and try to take a quick breath. You may want to close your mouth and pinch your nose to do this. That hurts around the sternum. The girl I mentioned earlier as having a visible shoulder jerk to a tiny trigger during a treatment probably had a very strong, physical jolt from a trigger. In treatment, under controlled circumstances when her trigger was presented minimally, we could see her shoulders jump almost an inch. I can only imagine how strong her reflex was in real life.

The second construct is that the physical misophonic reflex elicits a conditioned emotional response. The physical reflex is intrusive and difficult to ignore; even when a person tries to use a technique to avoid attending to the auditory stimulus, the physical reflex is perceived and elicits the emotional response.

There is still one more connection to add to our drawing of misophonia. The figure below shows the development of a direct connection between the misophonic trigger and the emotional response. This is a *secondary process*. In some cases, the patient has both an emotional response and a physical response to the very weak trigger used in the Neural Repatterning Technique (NRT) treatment (to be discussed later). The directly elicited emotional response is a secondary process because in most cases there is first a clear physical reflex which occurs independently of the emotional response during the NRT treatment.

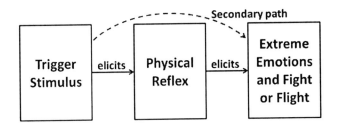

Benefits of Understanding the Misophonic Physical Reflex

Viewing misophonia as a physical reflex may help you manage your emotions. People have told you to just stay calm. You tried, but could not. People have told you that it's all in your head. When you have been angry at the person making your trigger sounds or sights, you have probably had horrible thoughts directed toward that person. You thought things that were completely inconsistent with your character. Many people with misophonia think about physically hurting the person making the triggers. You may have even said or done things that you feel sorry for. Guilt (after you calm down) is a common emotion for people with misophonia.

With misophonia, anger is not a choice. It is jerked out of you, and the reason you cannot stay calm without proper treatment is that this physical reflex is an assault on you. You are being physically assaulted, but you're being assaulted by your lizard brain. The sound comes into the brain, is perceived by the lizard brain, which then zaps you.

The misophonia-anger and the urge to physically assault are consistent with research done with mice in an electrical cage, where you could electrify the floor and shock them. (I didn't do this research, so please don't blame me for cruelty to animals.) When the mice were shocked, they attacked the adjacent mouse even though the other mouse had not done anything. This is called *pain-induced aggression*.[14] Essentially you're getting zapped or whacked, and that produces your anger response. The emotions are so enormous that you may not recognize the shock itself, but it is there. It is what kicks off your misophonic emotions.

So what can you do? First, be kind to yourself. Beating yourself up because you had horrible feelings toward another person doesn't help your misophonia. If you become physically or verbally abusive when triggered, you need to make a plan to avoid being triggered and a plan for what you will do when you are triggered.

Second, try thinking of your misophonic reaction as coming from your lizard brain, not from the person making the trigger. Misophonia *is* all in your head and it is extremely real. Your lizard brain is biting you. Look as the attack as coming from within. It is your lizard brain reflex.

Third, identifying your physical reflex may allow you to respond to triggers in a way that can lessen the agony of the trigger, and slowly change your lizard brain so that future triggers are less severe. This only applies to specific reflexes, but maybe you have an easy reflex to work with. Also, recognizing your reflex can help you with other treatments, such as the NRT treatment or SRT hypnotherapy treatment. If nothing else, you will have a better understanding of what is happening in your body when you are triggered and why it makes you so darn mad.

Identifying Your Physical Reflex

Identifying your physical reflex is not something you can figure out by thinking about the way you have reacted to triggers. Probably nine out of ten of my patients cannot come close to identifying their physical reflex from their own life experiences with triggers. The emotional upheaval from triggers is too great and there are too many physical responses that occur because of the extreme emotions and the fight-or-flight responses. If you think your initial physical reflex consists of all of your muscles tightening, then I respectfully suggest that you are incorrect. Your reflex will be one or several specific muscles or sensations in your body.

To determine this initial physical reflex, do a science experiment. Get very relaxed and then listen to a very small trigger. To make it a small trigger, typically it needs to be short and quiet. If it is a visual trigger, then you would probably have to do that with a video recording. With a sound trigger you might be able to have someone make a single trigger sound from another room. You can also use an audio or video recording and limit the length of time of the trigger and the volume. The Misophonia Reflex Finder app is free and is very good for doing this. You want the trigger to be very short (less than a half second) and barely audible. Then you slowly increase the volume until you start to trigger. At the point where you first feel the trigger, you will probably be able to determine where in your body you feel the reflex. Sometimes the reflex can't be described clearly. One person said their heart bumped. She didn't have an increased heart rate, just a single bump. She also had another muscle jerk as her misophonia reflex.

Another person said, "It's like something is growing in my chest. I can't describe it better than that." Another person I worked with, who didn't think she had a physical reflex, tested her body using electromyography (EMG) system which measures muscle contraction and did not find any physical reflex. But when she used the Misophonia Trigger Tamer, she felt the muscles behind her ears jerking. Using the EMG system , she tested herself and verified that when she heard a little trigger, those muscles behind her ears jerked. That was her physical reflex, and it was barely noticeable.

I had another person who didn't think she had a physical reflex, but she went to a doctor whom I work with, and he saw the reflex. During the treatment process the doctor had to trigger her, and he could see a jerk in a muscle near her eye.

Some people cannot identify a physical reflex, even though they physically feel the trigger. If you feel that a trigger jars your body, then you have a physical reflex, even if you cannot identify the specific muscle that moves when you are triggered.

All the Steps

We can expand our graph for the misophonia reaction a bit more. The next figure shows the extreme emotional response and the accompanying physical response (stress response) as two boxes that are adjoining. Anytime you are feeling emotions, the emotions consist of two parts. One part is what is going on in your head – what you perceive as the feeling, along with thoughts about it. The other part is what is happening in your body. There are automatic responses for emotions. If you are angry, you will have tense muscles and increased heart rate. If you are happy, you will have more relaxed muscles and positive sensations in your body (we will use this to our advantage later). The last box, labeled Coping Behaviors, comprises the things you do after you are triggered. This includes things that will reduce the trigger, such as putting your hands over your ears, mimicking the trigger noise, ordering the offending person to stop, or running away from the trigger. We will talk more about changing our behavior in each of these boxes later. For now, we just want to recognize that they exist as different components of your misophonic response to triggers.

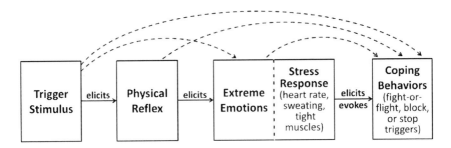

Summary

What is happening when you are triggered? It is not as simple as it seems to someone suffering with misophonia. Misophonia is really a two-step process.

Step 1: You hear or see a trigger. You perceive a trigger and you have an intrusive, physical reflex. This is an aversive, unpleasant, unwanted physical reflex.

Step 2: You feel the sensation of the physical reflex and instantly feel irritation or disgust. The physical sensation triggers your extreme emotions, and general physiologic (bodily) responses associated with emotional arousal including pressure in chest, head, and whole body; clenched/tightened muscles; sweaty palms; hard to breathe; and increased blood pressure and heart rate.

From my work with patients, I find that the way their physical reflex responds to treatment and to different strength of triggers is very consistent with the research on reflexes. This reflex is an acquired aversive physical reflex. An acquired reflex is also called a conditioned reflex or a Pavlovian reflex,[15] which we shall discuss in the next chapter.

10. Human Reflexes

Our reflexes are controlled by our Autonomic Nervous System (ANS)—the lizard brain. It controls the involuntary actions of the body. When there's a stimulus, there's a reflex response.

Some of your reflexes are things like sweating. Can you choose to sweat on command or not sweat? No. You go out into the bright light, and your pupil constricts. That's a reflex. All of your food processing is reflex action. Your heart rate is a reflex. The startle reflex is one we are familiar with. That's a reflex controlled by their lizard brain.

You have many reflexes that you were born with. These are innate or inborn reflexes, but we also develop reflexes throughout our lives, These are acquired reflexes. In fact, we begin to develop these reflexes the day we are born.[16] This process is called classical conditioning, or Pavlovian conditioning. As you may know, Ivan Pavlov was doing research on digestion and salivation using dogs in 1901, and he discovered that dogs were producing saliva before they ever got meat. So he designed an experiment to see if he could cause the dogs to produce saliva when he rang a bell.[17]

He gave them the meat, and they would produce saliva. At the same time, he rang a bell. Then he repeated the pattern of bell-meat-saliva, bell-meat-saliva. Then, bell-no-meat, and they still produced the saliva. What happened was there was a pairing of the bell and producing saliva because of the meat, so that after repeated pairings, the lizard brain learned that after the bell, its job was to produce saliva – and it did! The stimulus (the bell) and the response (producing saliva) locked together because the lizard brain observed what was happening over and over, so it decided to automatically fire off the reflex because of the stimulus. For years scientists thought it was the association of the bell and the meat that caused the reflex to develop, but recent research has shown that it was the association of the bell and salivation.[18]

Developing a reflex is a time sensitive process. To pick up this conditioned reflex response or acquired muscle reflex in humans, the critical timing is about half a second.[19] Suppose I had a bell (bing) stimulus and I poked you. Then we repeated bing-poke, where the poke comes half a second after the bell. You will start to flinch after the bing sound, even though I don't poke you. The timing needs to have the poke occur within two seconds after the bing sound, but half a second is the strongest time delay for acquiring a muscle reflex.

Usually with these conditioned reflexes, when you stop forcing the reflex response, the reflex dies out. In the bell-meat-saliva case, if you completely stopped providing meat, the reflex (producing saliva after the bell sound) would die out. But misophonia reflexes don't die out. I asked myself, "Why not?" The obvious answer is that there is something about experiencing a trigger that is causing the misophonia conditioned reflex to be strengthened. What appears to happen is that you are getting the trigger (i.e. the crunch sound) and you are having the reflex response. But then you are getting an emotional boost (which tightens the muscle more), so your lizard brain is comparing the crunch sound to this very tight muscle even though the lizard brain only tightened it halfway. So the lizard brain says, "Next time I should tighten the muscle harder." It is the effect of the emotional response after the trigger that causes the reflex to strengthen, so the misophonia reflex doesn't die out.

11. How Misophonia Develops

For many, a common sound suddenly starts making them angry. Several parents have said that all of a sudden their child exploded when they heard a certain sound. So misophonia may seem to happen automatically, like someone turned on a light switch, but data supports the view that misophonia actually develops in individuals through experience with the world around them. Research indicates that there are genetic factors that make one person more likely than another to develop misophonia.[20] But even though there are genetic factors, it still requires experience with the trigger sounds for misophonia to develop. But, somewhat surprisingly, it doesn't take long to develop a misophonic trigger.

I initially thought misophonia was caused by some traumatic event. I was wrong. People told me things like, "I sat by my grandmother in church and she was sniffling and her sniffling became my first trigger." Another person told me that they developed misophonia to their stepfather chewing his food, and that they dearly loved their stepfather (no trauma here).

A woman shared that when she was a little girl, her brother would smack his lips, and their dad would reprimand him. Brother smacks the lips, daddy yells at brother; brother smacks the lips, daddy yells at brother. So brother smacks, daddy yells, she cringes (a physical/emotional response). She was getting this physical/emotional response that went with her feeling, "Don't yell, Daddy." Her lizard brain began pairing the sound of her brother smacking his lips with her physical response that happened when daddy yelled, because she was a sensitive little girl. Her lizard brain learned to respond the her brother's lip smacking at the dinner table, but the first trigger she remembered was her brother smacking his lips while eating pancakes at breakfast. At the dinner table, her response was to daddy being upset, But at breakfast, daddy wasn't there. There was nobody to yell, but her little lizard brain heard that smack and jerked her body.

The following are some cases that illustrate how misophonia can develop.

John's Story

Consider the case of John, an individual I met at several misophonia conferences.[21] Now a middle-aged adult with misophonia, John recalled developing his first trigger. He shared a bedroom with his brother. John suffered from anxiety as a child. One night, he was unable to sleep. His brother had allergies and his breathing produced an audible nasal sound. After hours of hearing his brother breathe, John went to the couch and slept. From that night on, he was triggered whenever he heard his brother breathe. This type of experience, where one stimulus (sound) starts to cause a reflex response, is called Pavlovian or classical conditioning. The nasal breathing sound became associated with the physiological response[22] from the distress John experienced (i.e., specific contracted muscles) and/or the emotional distress experienced from anxiety, inability to sleep, and annoyance aroused by hearing the breathing sound. When he heard the sound later, it elicited the conditioned physical and/or emotional response. It seems that it is more the physical reflex response than the emotional response that becomes associated with the trigger (nasal breathing).

Carla's Story

Carla, age ten, came to the clinic with a primary misophonia trigger of her brother chewing. She said that when she heard the trigger, she felt immediate rage but no physical response. Carla often had conflict with her brother at the dinner table. Her mother reported that when arguing, Carla would stand, extend both arms, and demand that her brother stop staring at her. This was behavior that included tight arm and leg muscles. In this setting, she also heard the sound of her brother's open mouth chewing. At the clinic, a low-strength recorded trigger stimulus caused a visible jerk in Carla's arms and shoulders. When asked what she felt, she reported feeling the contraction of muscles in her arms and legs, but no anger, rage, disgust, or weaker precursors of these emotions. It seemed that the trigger stimulus caused the contraction of the same muscles that were contracted when she was arguing with her brother, which supports the hypotheses that misophonia develops as a Pavlovian-conditioned reflex and that the initial reflex response to a trigger stimulus is a physical reflex.

Connor's Story

Connor, age twenty-four, came to the clinic for treatment of misophonia with severe auditory triggers of chewing, sneezing, mouth breathing, and smacking lips, and a visual trigger of someone touching their glasses. He had developed misophonia while serving in the Marines in Afghanistan two years earlier. He reported that he also had a current diagnosis of PTSD. In Afghanistan, it was common to go on patrol as a squad, and upon returning to base to be in close quarters for eating. When tested for his initial physical misophonic reflex, his head visibly turned to the right, and he reported that he felt contraction of the muscles in his right arm and made a fist. The response was the same whether the trigger sound originated from his left or right side. This response seems similar to orienting to a sound of danger on his right side. The misophonic triggers did not elicit PTSD responses.

Bill's Story

Remember Bill's story that I mentioned briefly in Chapter 7? Bill was in good health, in his early thirties, with no history of mental health problems. He presented with misophonia trigger stimuli of mockingbird chirps and lesser triggers to some other birds. One year earlier, mockingbirds had built their nest near Bill's bedroom window. Mockingbirds have a unique characteristic of singing both day and night. The singing prevented Bill from sleeping and, over time, he developed a misophonic response to each of the five distinct calls of the mockingbird. Since then, he experienced an expansion of trigger stimuli to other (but not all) birds, though the misophonic response to other bird chirps was less severe. Bill's physical reflex was a "chill" on his upper arm and a sensation on the sides of his head.

Paul's Story

Consider the case of Paul, a middle-aged professional in good mental and physical health. He accepted a position in which he often received phone calls about problems he needed to handle. Paul developed a chest muscle contraction reflex to the default ringtone of the phone. It may be presumed that the chest muscle contraction was a physical response that accompanied the emotional reaction associated with the stress of the phone calls. He changed the ringtone to one which did not elicit the reflex; however, in time, the chest muscle contraction reflex developed to the new ringtone. He changed the ringtone several times, with the same result each time. Finally, he set his phone to vibrate only, and the reflex developed to the vibration ring of the phone. He also triggered to the ring of a phone on television, so it was clear that the sound elicited the reflex, independent of the caller or purpose of the call. In Paul's own words, "I hear the ring and my chest muscles jump, and I don't like it!" Paul's presenting problem was limited to his irritation with the physical reflex. He did not experience any emotion similar to those accompanying the stressful phone calls. This reflex did not restrict or impair his activity in any way, but was still an aversive reflex to a typically occurring sound. I propose that any aversive muscle contraction reflex to sound or other stimuli could be termed a misophonic reflex.

Misophonia – An Aversive Conditioned Reflex

These cases support the assertion that misophonia is an aversive Pavlovian conditioned reflex that develops when a person is in a state of distress and hears a repeating sound. In most of these cases, the sound could be a source or contributing factor for distress. In the case of Carla, it is not clear that the sound contributed to her distress, but the sound was being made by the person who was the source of her distress.

To develop the reflex, you have to have a state of distress and hear some repeating sounds. One way this happens is to experience distress where there is also an irritating sound that increases the distress.

Think of my open hand as a distress indicator: I got a little distressed (fist 25% closed), I heard a crunch (fist 50% closed), I heard the crunch again (fist 75% closed), I heard the crunch yet another time (fist very tight). I now have this extreme tight-muscle distress that is paired with the crunch sound. The next time I hear that crunch my lizard brain may not pull the muscle 100% tight, but it may pull it 25% or 50% tight. That jerk of the muscle to the trigger sound is misophonia.

The other possible situation is when you have tight muscles or a reflex for any reason and hear a repeating sound, which will create the acquired reflex in your lizard brain. So simply being put in distress while hearing a repetitive sound may also create misophonia.

Both of these scenarios are explained by the fundamental neurological process called *classical conditioning* that we discussed earlier in this chapter. Viewing misophonia as a conditioned reflex helps us understand how misophonia develops and how new triggers develop, including visual triggers.

12. How Triggers Spread

Triggers can spread like an infectious disease. If I kiss my grandkids that have a cold and then I kiss my wife, my wife ends up with a cold. The grandkids had contact with me, and then I had contact with my wife. So if I have a trigger sound and it comes in contact with some other sound, I can go away with two trigger sounds. This doesn't mean that you can pass a trigger on to another person. It means that anytime you are being triggered, and there is a repeating non-trigger sound or sight, you can develop a new trigger.

Here are some examples. Suppose you have a trigger to crunching, and while you are sitting at the dinner table being triggered you start noticing that the people are making sounds with their forks on the plates—the clicking. That clicking can become a trigger sound. You may trigger to the crunching at first, but you are also noticing that the person's sniffling at dinner table. Now you go away with crunching and sniffling triggers. You trigger to the crunching of one person but then you start noticing the eating sounds of other people at the table. You might then trigger to eating sounds from all of them, and then you start triggering to everyone in the world.

When a non-trigger sound occurs at the same time as a trigger sound, or while you are still upset from a trigger sound, the non-trigger sound can become a new trigger. The same thing is true with the visual triggers. Misophonia almost always starts with an auditory trigger, but any repeating visual image that occurs while you're being triggered can become a visual trigger. For example, consider gum chewing. You trigger to the popping sound of the gum, and then you see the person's jaw moving. Seeing the person's jaw movement becomes a new trigger. When this happens, the jaw movement becomes an independent trigger. Even if you do not hear the sound of gum popping because you are wearing headphones or earplugs, seeing the jaw movement will still trigger you. In fact, a person with misophonia may notice a person in another car chewing gum. There is no sound, but they may trigger to the visual of their jaw movement.

Brent's Story

Brent, a middle-aged man, had several visual triggers. He reported that his physical response to triggers was a constriction of his intestines. In the early days of working with the Visual Trigger Tamer app, we attempted treatment of a visual trigger. Because he was using music for the positive stimulus, a chime was included prior to the trigger so he would know when to view the trigger video. When he heard the chime, he would look at his cell phone, and one-half second after the chime, he would see a very short clip of his visual trigger. He was cautioned to keep the trigger stimulus short so his misophonic response would be weak and brief. Obtaining a brief response was particularly difficult because the intestinal constriction would persist if the trigger was too strong. We hoped this would minimize the risk of the chime becoming a trigger. Brent reported that in an effort to speed the treatment's effect, he increased the trigger strength. When he did this, the chime began to elicit intestine constriction, so the treatment was halted.

We have since modified the Visual Trigger Tamer so that it uses ten different chimes (a variety of sound clips) to alert the user to view the phone, and we increased the delay from one-half second to four seconds. However, in this case, we accidentally demonstrated that we could create a new trigger by pairing a neutral sound (chime) with the trigger stimulus (video clip). This demonstrated developing a new trigger stimulus through Pavlovian conditioning.

Minimize Your Response

You want to avoid triggers. If you stay in a triggering situation, you are setting yourself up to get a new trigger. And if you can't avoid the trigger, sometimes you can minimize your response. These techniques will be covered in more detail in the treatment section, but at this point, I will briefly mention them. One way you can minimize your response is to reduce the trigger reflex response by using background noise—a box fan, noise machines, headphones, and behind-the-ear sound generators are all great for reducing the misophonia reflex response. If you can reduce the response, then you're far less likely to pick up another sound as a trigger, because you won't be so emotionally distressed and distraught from being triggered.

You can also reduce your emotional response by viewing the trigger as a physical reflex. Say, "Oh that's my little lizard brain nipping at me. It's not the other person attacking me." There was a case study with cognitive behavior therapy where the person was able to deal with triggers in a calm way and carry on with her life. She didn't like the sounds, but she overcame the emotional upheaval from triggers. If you do that, then you might not pick up new triggers.

Muscle relaxation can also help. If you relax your muscles instantly after being triggered, you can greatly reduce the anger and rage that comes from the Misophonia trigger.

What do you do when there's a trigger? As your first option, if you hear a trigger, then you need to be free to leave. For example, parents of kids with misophonia should remember that your child needs to be free to get up and move away from the dinner table without you saying, "Oh, again!" If you grumble or complain, your child is not really free to leave. Your child needs to be free to move away from the trigger.

You need to avoid and escape the triggers because tolerating the triggers will only make your misophonia worse. If you have misophonia, it's up to you to protect yourself. A person doesn't have to be screaming or yelling or complaining to be sitting there getting triggered. You know when you are being triggered, so move away from it. A great tool is the Bose QC20 (or 20i or the QC25) noise cancelling headphones. They are wonderful at blocking out trigger sounds. With these headphones, you can be in a trigger situation but not be triggered at all, especially if you play some white noise (or any kind of noise). Playing white noise through these headphones can completely eliminate your audio triggers. These headphones are unique in their ability to block out single occurrence sounds.

You should also do the things that will improve your overall wellness, such as getting sufficient sleep, eating properly, diet, exercise, and muscle relaxation practice. These things help your mood and wellbeing, and the better you are feeling the less your misophonia is going to impact you. The less it impacts you, the less likely you are to pick up new triggers.

There's a second way that you can get a new trigger, and it's the way you got your first trigger: by pairing the response of the distress situation with a repeating sound. This is for non-triggers. To reduce the distress when hearing that irritating sound, just think of the world around you as a noisy place. It's not a personal attack on you. It's just environmental noise. It is life going on around you. Those noises are positive to someone or something, so try to put a positive spin on it. Try to relax about it. A good example of this was my wife reacting to my electric toothbrush. Luckily she didn't develop misophonia from this, but she could have. I have used an Interplak electric toothbrush ever since my mother gave me one twenty years ago. My wife would beat me to bed and start relaxing and chilling out. She was trying to read and relax, and I was in the bathroom with that noisy toothbrush. She said to herself, "That's so annoying. I wish he'd stop. Why does he have to use that stupid toothbrush?" She was emotionally upset, and there was a physiological action occurring also. That's just the type of situation where a person acquires a misophonic trigger, but luckily she didn't. One day she thought, "Pam, it's just an electric toothbrush. Lots of people use an electric toothbrush, so if Tom wants to use one, he has every right to." After that it never bothered her again.

There's something about putting a positive spin on sounds that helps you let them go. As I mentioned before, there's something positive about a lot of these sounds, even if it is only positive to someone else. For example, the sound of someone eating a chip might upset you, but it might be their comfort food that somehow makes their world feel better. Think about it from their shoes, for their sake. Distract yourself. Sing a song, say a poem, squeeze an object, focus on wiggling your toes or something, but get your mind off the sound by doing something else. Relax your muscles, and if you can't relax or ignore it then you have to just escape—get away from it because distress plus a repeating sound is a way that you develop another misophonic trigger.

I have worked with a few people that have two misophonia reflexes. For example, their jaw would clench in response to sounds of eating, and their shoulders clench in response to sounds of typing. That means that they developed misophonia twice. Most people don't. Most people only develop it once, and then they pick up new triggers by pairing a new sound with a trigger sound. So try to lighten up when it comes to mildly irritating, non-trigger sounds.

My conclusion is this: Take good care of yourself. Take charge of your trigger sounds. Don't let them take charge of you, and don't feel that you have to stay and tolerate a trigger sound. If you stay and tolerate it then you are liable to go away with a new trigger sound, and you don't want to do that.

13. Talking about Misophonia

This chapter is about the language and the words we use to describe misophonia. One of the problems is that we typically describe triggers, how we feel, and how we react to those sounds in common language. The problem with this approach is that it miscommunicates horribly. We say things like, "I don't like that sound," "That sound really bothers me," "Those sounds upset me," "They annoy me" or "irritate me" or "distress me" or "bug me." Here's the problem: these are common words in the English language, and other people think they know what they mean. For example, you say, "I don't like that sound." Well, I don't like cooked turnips. Since I know what it means to not like something, I think that the way I feel about cooked turnips is similar to how you feel about crunching. I think, "Okay. I understand what you mean. You should just get used to it." But I'm clueless. Or if you say, "That sound really bothers me." Well, houseflies bother me. So I know what it means to have something that bothers you. So I think I understand what it means for you to get triggered. But I don't understand. I'm clueless still.

This is why I use the word "trigger." A particular sound "triggers" me.

The listener is going to think or say, "What? I don't know what you mean." Now they are starting to communicate, because the person really doesn't know what the trigger is like.

Or if you say, "Oh that sound is one of my triggers," or "That is one of my triggers," then they are going to say, "Oh, okay. It is something that I don't understand. It's not something that you just dislike." We all have to deal with things that we dislike. But it's a trigger, and triggers are completely different than things that we dislike.

When you're talking about your misophonia with a person who's close to you, you want to be careful to not attack the person. If you can make it impersonal a little bit, you're better off. So remember the sound is detected by your lizard brain and your lizard brain is the one that assaults you. It zaps you. It attacks you physically and emotionally. So avoid attacking the other person. Don't say, "You make me so mad, I want to…" or "I hate it when you chew like that." Try something like, "That sound really triggers me," or "I lose it when I hear that sound." You're talking about you and a sound, not the other person. When I hear your eating, it triggers me. Remember it's a reflex. The other person isn't physically hurting you. It's your lizard brain that you want to be mad at.

When describing misophonia so that others might understand, call it a neurological condition, neurological disorder, or a reflex disorder. Say, "I have a neurological condition called misophonia, where certain common sounds trigger a reflex. The reflex is very unpleasant and it causes extreme negative emotions. In fact, getting triggered is like a physical and emotional assault. It's like getting slapped [poked with a stick, electrical shock, or zapped with a cattle-prod]." Choose the phrase you like, depending on what you experience when you hear a trigger. And you might say, "When I'm triggered, I can't concentrate on anything else because of the extreme emotions." That is a fairly accurate and understandable way to describe misophonia, and much more informative than just saying, "I hear those sounds and I get angry!" People don't really relate to that. But everyone knows what a reflex is and what a reflex does to you.

Sometimes I write letters of accommodation to employers or schools, and this is how they sound: "It's my professional opinion that John has a neurological condition known as misophonia or selective sounds sensitivity syndrome. Because of this condition, when he hears a trigger sound he experiences involuntary muscle reflexes and the tightening of the muscles. There are many sounds in his life that are trigger sounds." And then I give examples. I also work with the individual to try to determine their physical reflex, because it is easier to understand misophonia if you describe the physical component of it.

I might write, "When the sound is detected by his autonomic nervous system (ANS), the ANS quickly constricts muscles in his neck and shoulders," or whatever the individual's physical reflex is. "This is much like he's receiving an electrical shock. This reaction makes it difficult for him to stay in such an environment where he is repeatedly receiving electrical shocks." By reading such a statement, people understand that misophonia is a neurological condition and that it is a reflex. My clients have usually been successful in getting their schools and employers to make accommodations for them.

14. Management Techniques

As presented here, a management technique is one that will reduce the impact of the misophonia on the person's life, but will not change the fundamental reflex reactions of misophonia. Good management techniques can greatly reduce the severity rating of misophonia for an individual. Generally, management techniques are the first step to treating misophonia because they provide immediate relief. In many cases, only management techniques are used, because treatments for misophonia have sporadic results and the treatment effect may not last.

General Health and Wellness

It is almost a universal observation among my patients that when they are feeling good, triggers don't bother them as much as when they are feeling bad. Their general level of health and wellness is inversely related to the severity of their misophonia. This is not to say that someone who has excellent health and wellness cannot have extremely severe misophonia--they can. But it says that for any person with misophonia, when they feel bad, their misophonia is worse.

Some find that even moderate alcohol consumption makes their misophonia worse the next day. Others find a similar effect from eating too many sweets or carbs. I have seen the question posted on a Facebook group regarding the effect of a particular food on misophonia. If there is a food that your body does not tolerate well, then that food will make your misophonia worse. If you are lactose intolerant, then drinking milk will make your misophonia worse. If you have a slight allergy to gluten, then eating wheat products will make your misophonia worse. But you should not expect that because one person stopped eating carrots and their misophonia improved, that the same effect will work for you.

In general, the things that make a person feel better, like regular exercise, good sleep, a balanced diet, and so forth, will improve your misophonia. Take good care of yourself. You will improve your health and reduce your misophonia. It is a double benefit.

There was an interesting comment on a Facebook group by a person who had a significant improvement in her misophonia after taking a magnesium supplement. Many others reported trying magnesium supplements in various dosages, but it had no effect on their misophonia. Correspondence with the person who made the initial post revealed that she also suffered from chronic pain due to a complication from a broken leg. The magnesium supplement minimized her chronic pain, and when the pain was greatly reduced, her misophonia was also greatly reduced. It is likely that the magnesium supplement worked directly on her leg pain, and the reduction in pain decreased her misophonia.

Remember that misophonia includes a physical reflex. If her physical reflex jerked her body and caused a bit of pain, then reducing that pain source would greatly reduce the severity of her misophonia. I had a similar experience with my wife when she had chronic back pain. When I was driving the car, any little bump would cause her pain, and I heard about it (to say it nicely). Once her back felt better, she did not "appreciate" the bumps of the car, but they were no longer a big deal.

Avoid and Escape Triggers

Many people with misophonia are (or at some point have been) encouraged to be tough and put up with triggers. Misophonic people (especially children) don't want to be isolated, and they want to stay where the action is, even with the triggers. Parents or significant others have told them that they should ignore the triggers. Often those with misophonia don't want to cause trouble, and so their first approach to triggers it to do nothing but try to tolerate them. The desire to tolerate being triggered may stem from the hope that they will get used to the trigger, and that they will acclimate to the trigger as a person does many other stimuli. But a person does not habituate to triggers. With repeated episodes, the distress becomes greater and greater rather than smaller and smaller. A common response on the Misophonia Coping Survey, which I ask my new patients to fill out, is that they "leave the room after attempting to tolerate the sound." Often, this response is rated higher than "immediately leave the room to escape the sound."

The overall severity of a person's misophonic response is often based on the severity of a single trigger experience plus the number of triggers experienced per day. Other than trigger stimuli, a person with misophonia does not have unpleasant responses to sounds or sights. In fact, if you magically transported a misophonic person to a world where their triggers never occurred, they would perceive their self as no longer having misophonia. So my first rule of misophonia management is to reduce the number of triggers a person experiences per day. We will discuss several ways to do this below.

Being triggered is not a good thing, because it makes the misophonia response worse. It actually does it in two ways. First, it strengthens the actual reflex that hits you (that you feel) when you are triggered, and second, whenever you are being triggered, any repeating sight or sound in the environment can become a trigger. You don't want a stronger response to triggers, and you don't want any new triggers, so you want to avoid getting triggered. If you are in a trigger situation, you want to escape, get away, move away, or ask them to stop, but you really do not want to tolerate full strength, real-world triggers.

Family Trigger Management Plans

I recommend sharing the inconvenience and sacrifice that comes from changing family routines so that the misophonic person is not triggered. The misophonic person did not choose this condition—it happened to them. It is a bit like having a family member confined to a wheel chair. It affects everyone, but the family works together to make accommodations. So if a child has misophonia, and the father is the only trigger person, then a variety of schedule changes are possible that excludes the possibility of having the father chewing in the presence of the misophonic child.

It is important to make the plan with the misophonic individual. That may be difficult for children, who may be unwilling to follow such a plan. That is a different matter, but a plan is needed, and then the parents can calmly follow the plan and encourage the child to do likewise. This is also true for husbands and wives. Make a plan, and realize that being triggered is not a choice. Although it is not easy, try to not take it personally.

Add Sound to Your Environment and Ears

We find that the misophonic trigger response is more intense when the trigger sound is the only noise. We have all heard the saying, "It's so quiet you can hear a pin drop." When it's quiet, your auditory system essentially turns up the input sensitivity setting, making sounds seem louder. So a soft trigger will be perceived as louder, and the louder or stronger a trigger is, the stronger the misophonic reflex response.

Also, when it's quiet, a sound stands out more. They are easier to pick out because there are no other sounds competing with them.

Finally, the offending sound has higher fidelity or clarity. If there are other sounds, then the sounds are mixed together, and the clarity of the trigger sound is reduced. Reducing the clarity of the trigger can prevent the misophonic response or can minimize the response.

Audiologists - Misophonia Management Protocol

To reduce the misophonic response, avoid silence. To do this, you can add background noise to your life. Audiologist Martha Johnson developed this method of treating misophonia a number of years ago that does just this. She calls it the Misophonia Management Protocol (MMP)[23]. This is probably the most common management technique for misophonia. In addition to adding background sound, this protocol also recommends six to twelve weeks of therapy (CBT, DBT, or whatever you like) to help you change the negative thoughts about the trigger sounds and develop coping techniques. To add noise to your room, you can use something like a box fan running in the room. A box fan is a great noise generator. It is the cheapest and noisiest fan you can buy, costing less than twenty dollars in the USA. You can also use a white noise device such as the DOHM or LectroFan. Each is about the size of a stack of CDs. The DOHM is actually a fan in a box. It has two speeds and adjustments for volume and pitch. The LectroFan is an electronic noise generator, and it has ten fan sounds, ten other noises, and a volume control. The LectroFan currently has a higher rating on Amazon.com, and uses less power, but DOHM is very popular with people with misophonia. I don't have a recommendation of one over the other. You might want to have several of these devices so that you can keep them where you need them, such as in your kitchen, in your living room, and in your bedroom. You want to have sound everywhere you might hear triggers.

Box Fan

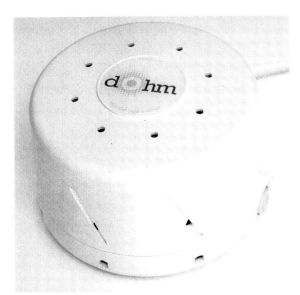

Dohm White Noise Machine

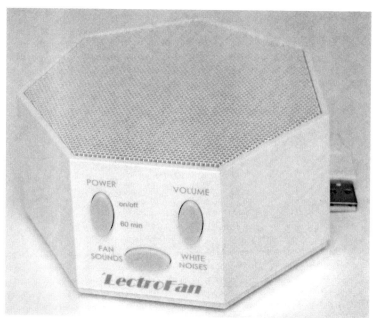

LectroFan White Noise Machine

You can also use the TV or music for background sound, but it is not as beneficial as the fan or noise. Music or TV sound varies in volume and the sound is not as effective at blocking or muting the trigger. If you have a sound system, then you can use a white noise app through a smartphone that is connected to your sound system, or you can use recorded white noise, pink noise, or rain sound. What you use depends on what you like and what is the most helpful for you.

An audiologist can supply can supply a personal sound environment. They provide a sound generator that goes behind the ear. These cost from $1,800 to $4,000 for a pair. Many people really love their sound generators. The devices look like a tiny hearing aid, but are programmed to emit the type of noise you like. Here is a picture of one:

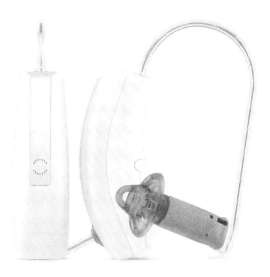

Widex Sound Generators

They are small and discreet. They are even invisible for a teenager wearing their hair forward. Even for guys with short hair, they are barely noticeable. These devices are also called masking devices. You should ask about these before going to see an audiologist because many audiologists and hearing aid centers do not sell them. These devices are commonly used to treat tinnitus, so any audiologist who provides treatment for tinnitus should be familiar with sound generators or masking devices.

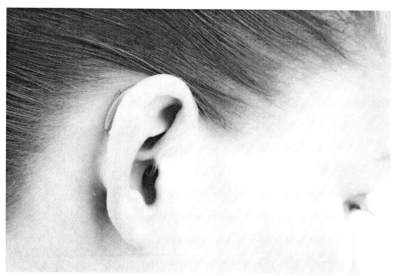
Widex Sound Generator, almost invisible.

When wearing a sound generator, you will still be triggered, but the trigger may be greatly reduced so it doesn't overpower you. You may be able to handle it without getting upset. Dr. Johnson's data on her patients showed that adding nondescript sound reduced the severity of a person's misophonia. It generally made their life livable. So getting some sound into your home, getting noise into your rooms, and adding noise directly to your ears is a very positive misophonia treatment for many people. About 60% of the people that went in to see Dr. Johnson ended up using (and liking) the little behind-the-ear sound generators. You can try it out if you want by using your iPod and open ear headphones, which cost less than twenty dollars, if you get the Sony Sport brand.

Dr. Johnson reported that the Misophonia Management Protocol had an average effect of reducing the severity of a person's misophonia from severe to moderate or moderate to mild.[24] Based on the sum score of the Misophonia Assessment Questionnaire (MAQ), she classified patients as having severe, moderate, or mild misophonia. The MAQ has twenty-one questions on a scale of zero to three. The maximum score is sixty-three. Twenty-two to forty-two was moderate. Above forty-two was severe, while below twenty-two was mild. It's not a cure, but it makes life much better and is really a very good thing. It's also important to note many people have an immediate benefit from the added sound or noise, which is helpful for a person suffering from misophonia.

A critical aspect of this treatment is to have your ear exposed so you can still hear, and thus you need to understand that you are still going to get triggered. The severity of your trigger response should be reduced, so you'll feel a lower level response. You can increase the volume of your background noise—of your iPod or of your sound generator—when you need to, such as when it's a higher trigger situation or you are just more sensitive. You can decrease the volume of the noise when it's not needed.

Help with Headphones

You can try out the sound component of the MMP using open ear headphones, which cost less than twenty dollars. You can get a noise app to run on your phone, iPod, or tablet. One of my favorite white noise apps is White Noise by TMSOFT.

As of this writing, you can get the free version with ten sounds or pay two dollars for the full version with forty sounds. You can also add your own sounds and create custom sound mixes. I highly

White Noise

By TMSOFT

Open iTunes to buy and dov

View in iTunes

$1.99

Category: Health & Fitness

recommend the full version so that you can choose a noise sound that is best to block your triggers. This app runs on both Android and iPhone. You can buy open-ear headphones such as one of the Sony Sport Headphones. There are several models. If you Google Sony Sport Headphones you'll find them. (Two current models of these headphones are MDR-J10 and MDR-AS200.)

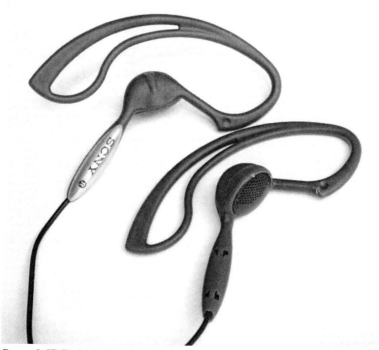

Sony MDR-J11 Headphones

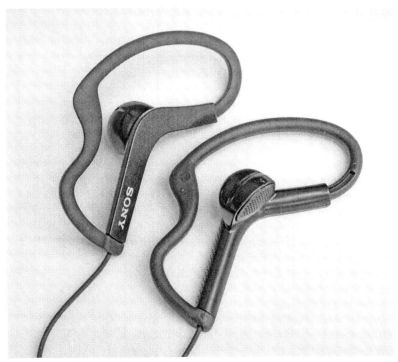
Sony MDR-AS200 Headphones

These headphones clip over the ear. The nice thing about these is the speaker does not plug your ear canal, so you can still hear. This way you can hear a mix of the sound from the noise app and the sound around you.

Do you remember Sony Walkman headphones? They were the perfect open ear headphone. Sony doesn't make them anymore, but Sonxtronix has recently made them available (Sonxtronix XDR-8000). These are very comfortable and leave the ear canal open to hear normally.

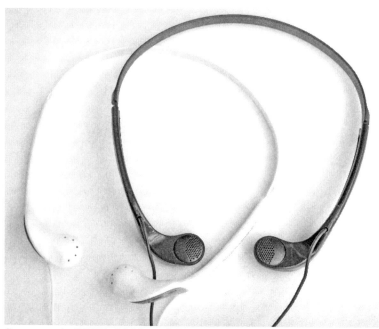

Sonxtronix XDR-8000 and XDR-8001 Headphones

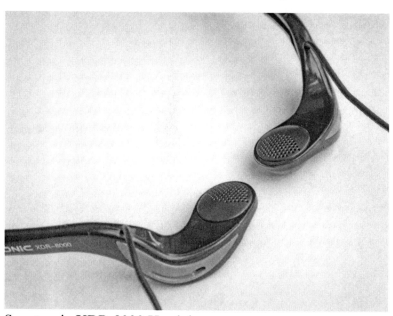

Sonxtronix XDR-8000 Headphones

This is the "poor man's" version of a personal noise generator. You can increase the noise on your iPod high enough that it reduces your reflex response to your trigger sounds. In a trigger situation you can raise the volume to help block them out, and reduce the noise at other times. This really does reduce the intensity of your misophonic response, so the triggers don't hit you so hard. You can also use the Bose QC20 noise cancelling headphones by turning on the "Aware" feature, which lets you hear sound around you as if you had no headphones on. It passes the outside sound through instead of cancelling and blocking outside sound.

If you don't have an iPod touch or smartphone, then you can buy a cheap Android phone, like the Kyocera Event. The Event costs less than thirty dollars and runs Android 4.0, so it can run all the newest white noise apps. You don't need to activate it for this use, so there is no monthly fee.

At the dinner table you can have some tricky situations using the Misophonia Management Protocol (MMP) and sound generators, or even with headphones that totally block the sound because you may have visual triggers. Headphones don't block out visual triggers, and visual triggers are standalone, meaning once a visual trigger develops, a person is triggered without hearing the sound. So you can block all sound, and the person may still be triggered by seeing jaw movement or a person putting food in their mouth.

I worked with a family who had a child that was triggered by the sight of her parent chewing. They wanted to have dinner together, so they all sat on the same side of the table, because that prevented the visual triggers and allowed them to eat together. It may seem a bit odd, but it is much better than the child eating in the room by herself.

In summary, misophonia management with sound is the quickest intervention. It can give you an immediate reduction in the trigger reflex. You may completely block the trigger if you turn the sound up and wear earbuds or some other headphones. This allows you to greatly reduce or eliminate triggering in certain situations. You should add noise to any setting where you will be triggered because the added noise reduces the overall severity of the trigger response. While using noise to reduce the severity of the trigger makes life more bearable, it's not a cure. It doesn't cause the reflex to die out. It's a way of dealing with misophonia as a chronic condition; and remember, it has no effect on visual triggers, so you still have to deal with those.

Earplugs and Noise Cancelling Headphones

Let's start with the warning about the over-use of earplugs. Your brain seeks auditory input, and adjusts based on your environment. When you starve your brain for stimulation from sound, your brain will become more sensitive to soft sounds. Because misophonia generally includes triggers of soft sounds, excessive use of earplugs increases your sensitivity to many trigger sounds. So beware: Do not use earplugs as an everyday method for blocking out triggers. If you need to block trigger sounds for prolonged periods of time, use noise cancelling headphones and play music or noise so you provide continual stimulation for your auditory system.

Appropriate Use of Earplugs

You may want to use earplugs at night, or in specific, short-term situations. For example, when you are taking an exam, earplugs are appropriate.

When you use earplugs, make sure that they fit completely into the ear. When I use them, they are so deep that I have to pick the earplug out using my fingernail. Any part of the earplug that is outside your ear canal is material that is wasted. Only the material within your ear canal blocks the sound.

There are two common types of earplugs. One is a molded foam, conical shape, with a rounded tip. These are often brightly colored. The second type is a foam cylinder punched out of a sheet of material. These are generally beige or yellow. The molded foam can be reused more times, but hurt my ears when I sleep with them because they push harder against the ear canal. The punched cylinder types are my favorites, but can only be used a few times.

Noise Cancelling Headphones

Headphones can be helpful at blocking triggers. Although kids would prefer to listen to music through headphones, music does not block triggers as well as noise. Music has loud, soft, and even silence between songs. Noise is constant. Noise tends to include sounds that have more similarity to triggers than does music.

A great misophonic management tool is the noise cancelling Bose QC20 or QC25 headphones. The QC20 was the first headphones designed to cancel out single occurrence sounds, such as speech. All noise cancelling headphones are good at blocking background noise, but it is the triggers that we are trying to block. Bose headphones are excellent at cancelling out single occurrence sounds. The QC20 is an earbud style, but fits just outside the ear canal and plugs it, making it very comfortable for extended use. The Bose QC25 is equally good and is an over-the-ear style. I don't know of any other noise cancelling headphones that work as well as these Bose models. These headphones will virtually eliminate sound triggers when used in noise cancelling mode, and while playing a noise app. They do this without blasting so loudly that you may damage your ears. Unfortunately, they have no effect on visual triggers.

The Bose headphones are expensive, but you get what you pay for. An economical alternative to completely block auditory triggers is to use a combination of earplugs and over-the-ear headphones blasting noise or music. The earplugs prevent damage to your ears from the loud noise, and the combination completely eliminates ambient sounds. This way your brain has auditory input, but all triggers are blocked. You can also accomplish the same thing using earbuds and earmuff style hearing protectors. Either combination gives great noise isolation at a low cost.

Daily Muscle Relaxation Practice

Progressive Muscle Relaxation (PMR) and Applied Relaxation are methods of managing and treating your misophonia. PMR consists of daily practice, taking ten to twenty minutes, in which you develop the skill to relax your muscles. To get the benefit from this technique, you need to do the PMR routine every day for several months. It is not quick, but the benefits can be enormous. In fact, it is possible to virtually cure misophonia using muscle relaxation. But muscle relaxation is a skill, and a skill can only be learned with practice.

This technique will help you manage your misophonia in two ways. First, practicing PMR every day will improve your overall level of health and wellbeing, which will reduce your misophonia. This benefit can occur very quickly, especially if you have trouble sleeping. Second, practicing muscle relaxation will develop a skill that you can use immediately after you are triggered to greatly reduce the anger response that is typical of misophonia. Third, relaxing before and during a trigger situation can greatly reduce the physical and emotional response to the triggers. The benefits of muscle relaxation as a treatment will be discussed in the next chapter.

Overview of PMR and Applied Relaxation

PMR was developed in the early 1920s by an American physician named Edmund Jacobson to help patients with stress and anxiety. It is known as Differential Muscle Relaxation in the U.K.

Everyone's heard the phrase, "I feel very tense." The word "tense" relates to the muscle tension. Originally PMR was a series of tightening and relaxing two hundred different muscle groups in the body. But since that time we found that we get the same benefit by working fifteen to twenty skeletal muscle groups[25] Researchers have demonstrated that individuals who practice PMR develop increased control of skeletal muscles, including a reduction in muscle tension during stressful events.[26] This means that a person with misophonia will be better able to relax their muscles after being triggered. Their muscles will not stay 100% relaxed, but the more they can relax their muscles, the more it will minimize their misophonic reactions. It will also help a person calm down at a faster rate, so maybe they can calm down in five or ten minutes instead of an hour.

There are many reliable sources of information about PMR.[27] Daily PMR has been shown to be beneficial in treating anxiety disorders and improving well-being because it produces a state of deep relaxation. PMR is just one way of obtaining a state of deep relaxation.[28] With a physiological state of deep relaxation you will have a decrease in your heart rate, in your respiration rate, in your breathing, your blood pressure, tension in your skeletal muscles, your metabolic rate or your oxygen consumption, and you will actually have a reduction in your analytical thinking.

Daily deep relaxation offers a variety of benefits. Here are a few that are common as a result of daily progressive muscle relaxation:

• Reduced generalized anxiety.
• Less accumulation of stress.

• Increased energy and productivity.
• Improved concentration and memory.
• Better sleep.
• Reduction of psychosomatic disorders such as high blood pressure, migraines, headaches, asthma, and ulcers.
• Increased self-confidence, reduced self-blame, and increased awareness of feelings/emotions.

The reason you have an increased awareness of your feelings is that we perceive our feelings from our body in a number of ways. There are different states of muscle tension when you feel calm, relaxed, or happy versus when you are tense or angry. If your muscles are always tense, you trick your body into believing you are agitated. By practicing any form of daily deep relaxation, you can calm your muscles and then have an increased—and more accurate—awareness of your mood and feelings.

Applied Relaxation is relaxing your muscles, without tightening them. [29] You need to practice this also. After you have practiced PMR a minimum of ten times, take two minutes to relax each muscle group sequentially, in the same order as PMR, but without first tensing them. Step through each muscle group, similar to the way you did PMR, but simply relax each group. For example, relax your fists for five to ten seconds, then your biceps, then your triceps, your forehead, and keep going through each of the muscle groups that you used for PMR. Do this at least once a day.

The final phase develops the skill of relaxing all muscles simultaneously. Sit or lie comfortably and say to yourself, "Relax." Focus on relaxing all your muscles. Then say, "Relax" again, and relax all your muscles even further. Scan your body and release any muscle that still has tension. Hold this fully relaxed state for one minute.

One researcher found that it took up to a dozen hour-long sessions to learn this skill, including the progressive muscle relaxation component.[30] You can practice this skill on your own or with a therapist. The biggest problem with learning PMR and Applied Relaxation is practicing it every day. To be successful, you will probably need to incorporate this activity into your schedule. Set a fixed time each day for your PMR exercise. Also, plan times for you to practice both types of Applied Relaxation. This will take a great deal of effort, but the benefit is worth it, especially when you graduate to using muscle relaxation as a treatment for your misophonia.

Muscle Relaxation as a Management Technique

At the 2013 Misophonia Conference for Audiologists, I met a man who used muscle relaxation to eliminate his anger after being triggered. He was about 50 years old, and developed proficiency in progressive muscle relaxation (PMR) as a treatment for his general anxiety as a teenager. For many years he had relaxed his muscles immediately after trigger stimuli to suppress his emotional response.

Although he initially practiced and learned relaxation using PMR, the technique he described (relaxing all his muscles after a trigger) was Applied Relaxation. Simply relaxing after the trigger prevented rage. We find that anger has a physiological component to it of tense muscles. And so if you're angry (mentally), but your muscles are relaxed, it plays a trick on your brain. Those are inconsistent events. Tight muscles go with anger, while relaxed muscles go with calm. So by just willfully relaxing your muscles after a trigger, you can drastically reduce the anger that comes from a misophonic trigger.

If you are in a trigger situation, and your initial physical reflex is a skeletal muscle, then relaxing your muscles before a trigger will reduce the strength of your physical misophonic reflex and therefore will reduce the intensity of your misophonic emotions that typically follow a trigger. Practice and learn PMR and Applied Relaxation and give it a try. You will be glad you did.

Guidelines for Progressive Muscle Relaxation[31]

It's best to do it twice a day if you can, preferably morning and night, especially for the first week to ten days. Once a day is sufficient, but it will take longer for you to see the benefit of PMR.

You need a quiet location with no distractions and twenty to thirty minutes to do Progressive Muscle Relaxation. To start, it's going to take at least twenty minutes. Once you are proficient, you can complete the exercise in ten minutes.

It's best if you do it at a regular time, and on an empty stomach. You need to find a comfortable body position using a sofa, a bed, a recliner, or lay on the floor. Loosen any tight clothing. Try not to worry or think about anything else. You want to have a more passive, detached attitude of just being there and letting it happen. You have to do the work, but you need to be unemotionally involved. You want to be more of an observer than concerned or thoughtful about the exercise. Observing the way your muscles feel is an important part of PMR.

To do a PMR session, start with a few deep breaths. Then you tense a muscle group for seven to ten seconds. You don't want to strain, but you want to hold it really tight. You concentrate on the muscle. Feel and visualize the tension, then abruptly relax that muscle. Keep it relaxed it for fifteen to twenty seconds, and feel the limpness and lack of tension. Note the difference between tense and relaxed. Then, repeat this for each muscle group in your body that you're going to use for this exercise.

Here's a handy guide.

1. Take three slow, deep abdominal breaths. Imagine the tension going away as you breathe out.
2. For each of the following muscle groups, tighten the muscle for seven to ten seconds and focus your attention on how the muscle feels when it is tight. Then relax the muscle for fifteen to twenty seconds and feel the limpness of the muscle. Pay attention to how the muscle feels tight vs. limp to grow the neuron connections to willfully relax these muscles.
   – Fists
   – Biceps (fists to shoulders)
   – Triceps (extend arms straight out sideways)
   – Forehead (raise your eyebrows)
   – Around eyes (eyes shut)
   – Jaw open (wide open)
   – Neck (head back)
   – Shoulders (shoulders toward ears)
   – Shoulder blades (try to touch them together)
   – Chest (deep chest breath, release this one slowly)
   – Stomach (suck stomach in)
   – Lower back (arch back – but not if it is painful)
   – Buttocks (pull them together)
   – Thighs (tighten all muscles)
   – Calf muscles (pull toes up)
   – Feet (curl toes downward)
   – Scan your body for tension. Repeat any tight muscle groups.
3. Imagine a wave of relaxation slowly going through your body from head to toe.

Progressive Muscle Relaxation is a powerful treatment for misophonia, and that's why you should be doing it. The main benefit for misophonia is that it lets you relax your muscles on demand, which can only be done after you have developed the skill of relaxing your muscles. It takes about two weeks to learn the skill of relaxing your muscles, and even then, you will get better with practice. Instead of PMR (Progressive Muscle Relaxation), maybe you should think of it as MRP (Muscle Relaxation Practice). That is what you are doing each day: *practicing* to relax your muscles. You are making the neuron connections in the brain so that when you say, "relax," you can actually relax your muscles. The ability to do this doesn't just happen; it's an acquired skill. It is not a concept. So you have to plan on doing MRP at least fourteen times to make sure that you have started to develop the actual skill. Then when you're triggered you want to just relax.

Remember, it also improves your overall general well-being, and that reduces the impact and the severity of your misophonia. Another great benefit is that once you've learned this technique, you can also use it when you know you're going to be triggered. This is especially beneficial if you have an initial physical misophonia reflex that is a skeletal muscle. If you relax those muscles before being triggered, then it will help to change your little lizard brain and reduce your misophonia. There is at least one case of a person who eliminated his misophonia this way.

Go to misophoniatreatment.com and look up the Progressive Muscle Relaxation guided audios. There's one that is twenty-five minutes long. It's from Dartmouth University, and I suggest that you try that one at least one time. There is another one by Arizona State University that is fifteen minutes long, and you should try that at least once. Use one of the guided audios for the first week, because they emphasize the mental thoughts of focusing on the tightness and focusing on the relaxation that is critical to developing the neuron connections so you can relax your muscles on demand. If you're triggered by the voice on the PMR guided audio, you can use the script for PMR that is on the same web page and one of the last two audio files. These only have timing chimes—no words. If you want to use one of the shorter audio files once you know what you are doing, go ahead. Practice muscle relaxation twice a day if you want to see the improvement quickly, but practice it at least once every day

No Threat, But Thank You

"No threat, but thank you" is a coping skill that may seem a bit silly, but it works for many people. But first, a quick review of some of the misophonia neurology.

At the top we have our cerebrum, our thinking brain. In the middle we have our emotional brain, the limbic system. Down at the bottom of our brain is the brainstem—the autonomic nervous system, our lizard brain. It's that lizard brain reflex that controls the misophonia.

Now, your lizard brain may cause you to have a misophonic response, but it's also your best friend. Your lizard brain controls all the automatic processes in your body. It keeps you alive. It does your automatic breathing, blinking, adjusting your body temperature, sweating or shivering, and other blood flow changes that adjust your body temperature. It does all your food processing, even swallowing; without your lizard you would swallow and food would stop at the top of your esophagus because the lizard brain does the reflex that massages the esophagus and pushes the food down into the stomach. One of your lizard brain reflexes that's a lot like a misophonia reflex is the startle response. You pop a balloon behind someone and they will jump—that startle response is coming from their lizard brain.

Now, your lizard brain helps you adapt to the world around you. It really balances things out by predicting how the body should respond based on its past experience. So, for example, if a waiter puts a large plate of pasta in front of you, before you ever start eating your lizard brain says, "I have seen this situation before and I know it this is going to require a lot of insulin to handle this pasta load so I am going to start producing the insulin now." This happens before you ever start eating based on the stimulus of having the pasta in front of you. Your lizard brain puts together sights and sounds in the environment and physical responses.

Think of your misophonic response to triggers as your lizard brain trying to warn you of a threat or some danger on your life. You hear this crunch and the lizard brain jerks your body (like a small startle reflex). It says, "Hey look out, danger, there's a threat."

Well, the trick is to have a conversation with your lizard brain. The long version sounds like this, "Lizard brain, I know you're trying to protect me. What you just heard was not a threat to my life, but thank you for trying to protect me."

You need to do that in a short version, something more like a factual statement, "not a threat" or "no threat" and then energetically, "but thank you!" Simply say, "No threat, thank you!" You may think it, but you need to think it with gusto. That "thank you" needs to be a strong "thank you" because what I think is happening is that "thank you" is a positive trigger. It triggers a lizard brain reflex.

Many times you've been exposed to a situation where something has happened that has been very positive and you said, "thank you." Your lizard brain heard the thank you and observed the positive physical conditions that you were experiencing at the moment, and it put the two together. So when you say, "thank you," it triggers a positive physical reflex like those previously paired with those words. I call it a gratitude reflex. So let's try this: say a nice strong "thank you," and then pause and see what you feel in your body. Ready? "Thank you." From that you may get a calm, peaceful feeling in your body that is quite the opposite of anger. And so this "thank you" reflex will overlay and squash the anger reflex.

A woman on Facebook wrote this;

"I must say, Tom Dozier, after watching your video from your conference that you shared [this was from the 2014 Misophonia Association Conference], I was shaking my head thinking, 'well, this is nonsense.' After being violent most of my sixty-one years, and feeling that isolation and loud televisions and earplugs were going to follow me all the way to the crematorium, I had an opportunity to use your lizard brain suggestion of telling myself that there is no threat, that it's okay. I was stuck in the car, next to my husband, on the way to the coast, facing three long hours of sniffling and crunching potato chips. I thought, 'What the heck, I will give ole Tom's advice a whirl.'

"Guess what? I suppose the old dog, new trick scenario works here. Much to my surprise I didn't feel like jumping from the car onto the freeway. I also had a chance to use it while my husband was snoring in the hotel. I did get up after an hour and get the earplugs, but I didn't feel as angry. Good for you, Tom! I advise anyone who suffers to just give this a try. It won't take the problem away, but then again, you probably won't be featured on *America's Most Wanted*."

So give it a try. Many say that they like this trick, while some don't. But what do you have to lose by trying? So when you are triggered, think quickly, "No threat, but thank you!" and see if it doesn't help that anger melt away.

Attitude

Maybe you have been told, "It's all in your head." When someone tells you this, they mean that you are imagining or making up misophonia. In this regard, they are very wrong. You are not making up misophonia. Misophonia is very real, but in reality it *is* all in your head—in your lizard brain, more specifically. It can be helpful to realize that your triggers are just that – *your* triggers. They are not evil sights and sounds that the whole world detests. They are normal, everyday occurrences that go unnoticed by 90% of people. But for you, those sights and sounds are your own hell. The triggers cause your lizard brain to respond, and your lizard brain literally bites you! It zaps you in some way. Viewing that "bite" or "zap" from your lizard brain as something your own brain is doing to you can be less disturbing than someone else attacking you.

If you have a sprained ankle, it hurts to walk on it. You feel pain with each step, but you don't feel anger with each step. Why? Probably because you know that the pain is originating in your body, from the injury, and not being caused by someone hurting you.

The same thing applies to misophonia. If you view misophonic triggers as the result of someone attacking you, then you will likely be more upset. If you view the triggers as something you need to cope with because you respond to the world differently, then you can focus on how you should be responding. That response should include the other techniques listed in this chapter, including muscle relaxation, putting on headphones, walking away, and other productive methods of managing your misophonia.

If you view triggers as others attacking you, then it's all their fault. They should not be causing the triggers; they should have better manners. They need to learn how to pick up their feet when they walk, and to breathe silently! But this attitude is one that is likely to cause you more resentment and feelings of victimization. When someone attacks you, it is natural to become angry. So instead of feeling like a victim who is being attacked, view your misophonia more like a sprained ankle. It hurts, but you can manage it.

I don't claim that this will make misophonia okay, or that misophonia will no longer be a problem if you have the right attitude. What I am suggesting is that your attitude may make a difference, and that it is one of many things that can reduce the severity of your misophonia.

504 Plan for Workplace and School Accommodations

The Americans with Disabilities Act provides for accommodations for students (504 Plan) and workers.

The US Department of Labor website says, "Under the Americans with Disabilities Act (ADA), an accommodation is considered any modification or adjustment to a job or work environment that enables a qualified person with a disability to apply for or perform a job. The term also encompasses alterations to ensure a qualified individual with a disability has rights and privileges in employment equal to those of employees without disabilities. The obligation to provide reasonable accommodations for job applicants or employees with disabilities is one of the key non-discrimination requirements in the ADA's employment provisions."

The ADA does not grant you the right to have your own office, but it does require your employer to provide reasonable workplace accommodations. For example, simply being able to wear headphones in the workplace, or have a telephone that allows you to use noise cancelling headphones, can make a great difference. You might ask yourself, "Can a deaf person do this job?" If the answer is yes, then you should be able to wear headphones all the time (even if your company has a policy that headphones are not allowed). You will need to help figure out what accommodations will help you.

Students with misophonia can often benefit from a 504 plan for school. If their misophonia affects them at school, a 504 plan will give their parents legal rights to advocate for accommodations on the child's behalf. A child is eligible for a 504 plan if their disability "substantially limits one or more major life activity."

Examples of these include learning, speaking, listening, reading, writing, concentrating, and caring for oneself. Misophonia definitely causes problems with concentrating.

The 504 plan needs to meet the requirement of providing a Free Appropriate Public Education, as required by the ADA. The following is from the government website http://www2.ed.gov/about/offices/list/ocr/504faq.html#skipnav2.

"The Section 504 regulations require a school district to provide a 'free appropriate public education' (FAPE) to each qualified student with a disability who is in the school district's jurisdiction, regardless of the nature or severity of the disability. Under Section 504, FAPE consists of the provision of regular or special education and related aids and services designed to meet the student's individual educational needs as adequately as the needs of nondisabled students are met." A 504 plan is different from an IEP. The main difference is that a 504 plan provides accommodations that mitigate the disability, where an IEP may require different educational services so ˙ ɘ child will meet minimum learning objectives. A 504 plan can be provided for an exceptionally bright student who may be making all A's but cannot concentrate in class.

The following are examples that seem to be reasonable accommodations for K-12 students:

1. That there is no eating, drinking, or gum chewing in the classes that she attends, and that this is enforced.
2. That he be allowed to leave a classroom without penalty. This is sometimes necessary when there are too many triggers occurring. When she leaves the class, she needs to have unrestricted access to a location that is free of trigger stimuli where she can calm down.
3. That he be allowed to use headphones and a noise generator app in class. This may reduce his ability to hear the teacher,

but it will often allow him to remain in class and do his work.

4. That he be allowed to use his headphones and noise generator in class during tests.
5. That he be provided a trigger-free location for testing, if needed.
6. That he be provided preferred seating to reduce his exposure to triggers.
7. That a transmitter/receiver set be provided so that the teacher can wear a microphone and the student can hear the lecture through headphones. (This is common for hard of hearing students.)

In many cases, a 504 plan is not required because the school cooperates on making accommodations. It is always better to get what you need through cooperation than to force the school through a 504 plan and threatened legal action, because the accommodations will likely be implemented more consistently if the school views them as necessary rather than an unreasonable request they are being forced to comply with.

A Few Tricks with Technology

Movie theaters are known to those with misophonia as a place of torture due to the munching of popcorn. But there is a simple trick to overcome this problem—ask for the headphones for the hearing-impaired. In some theaters, you will receive a pair of over-the-ear headphones with a built-in receiver. In others, you will receive a hand-held receiver and will need to provide your own headphones. Either way, you will have your own personal sound system. If you are extremely sensitive to the munching sound, then bring a pair of earplugs. You can wear the earplugs and then turn up the volume on your headphones. It is suggested that you sit in the center of the theater for the receiver to work best.

Hearing-impaired receivers are also available in many churches and university classrooms. The hand-held receiver seems to be more common at universities, and is also provided at my church. If you need to add noise to reduce the triggers of the person speaking, then you can use a splitter (in reverse) and add the sound of a noise app from your phone. This way, you get the benefit of reduced triggers from the speaker due to added noise, and isolation from triggers produced by those near you.

Technology today is marvelous. If you need noise cancelling headphones for your phone at work, speak up. There are many devices designed for those with hearing problems that will help block triggers around you.

15. Treatments

Let me begin by saying that in many ways, continued management of misophonia is a form of treatment of misophonia. For example, many who use sound generators are pleased with the reduction of misophonia, and so their pain of misophonia is greatly reduced. Therefore the Misophonia Management Protocol listed in the previous chapter might have also been listed here as a treatment. Additionally, the information on treatments presented below is based on my personal experience and available published research. Therefore, I discuss treatments I have worked with more extensively than those I have not due to the limited information on the others.

Progressive Muscle Relaxation and Applied Relaxation

[Note that this treatment is only for people who have an initial physical misophonic reflex that is a skeletal muscle, such as a clenching your fist or jerking your shoulder. If your physical reflex is internal, such as a stomach constriction or some movement in your chest cavity, then you cannot willfully relax those muscles and thereby reduce your misophonia reflex response.]

Relaxing your muscles immediately after a trigger (which is Applied Relaxation) can greatly reduce the anger response. Daily Progressive Muscle Relaxation (PMR) can also improve your general level of wellness and wellbeing, which leads to reducing your misophonia. Relaxing your muscles before you are triggered can change the connections in your lizard brain and slowly reduce the intensity of the misophonic physical reflex, thereby reducing the severity of your misophonia. Because of this, I include muscle relaxation both under misophonia management techniques and misophonia treatments.

The chapter on management techniques explains how to perform PMR. To use it as a treatment method, you need to become proficient in relaxing your muscles immediately, without first tensing them. Daily PMR builds the neuron connections needed to willfully relax skeletal muscles. You will likely need to do the PMR exercise every day for two weeks to begin to develop this control, but you may need to work for months to develop sufficient control to relax your muscles before and during triggers. You then need to practice Applied Relaxation and develop the skill of relaxing all your muscles quickly, without tightening them.

Triggers often come in groups, rather than a single trigger. A person sitting near you may be sniffling, crunching, or typing. These triggers, especially eating and typing, are almost continual. To change the connections in your brain that cause your misophonic reflex, you need to relax the muscle of your initial physical misophonic reflex before you are triggered. You can relax other muscles also, but the lizard brain learning (repatterning) comes from relaxing the muscle that is jerked by your lizard brain when you hear a trigger.

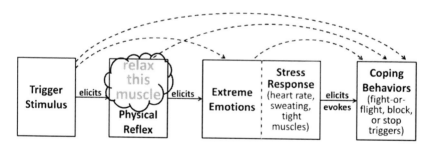

By relaxing the muscle that is jerked with the misophonic reflex, it will contract less, and almost immediately start to relax. During the critical "training" time, which is the first two seconds after the trigger, your lizard brain will detect a more relaxed muscle. Because of this, it will jerk the muscle slightly less the next time. Over time, the physical reflex will decay away. In order for this to happen, you need to be highly skilled in relaxing your muscle, and it takes practice to develop this skill. Because of this, you need lots of practice in PMR to develop the neuron connections needed to become a master muscle relaxer. You also need lots of practice of Applied Relaxation, which is relaxing your muscle on command, without tensing it. The most important muscle to learn to relax is the muscle of your initial physical misophonic reflex.

Relaxing your muscles before and during a trigger may seem like a little thing, but it's not: it's a powerful lizard brain training/changing activity. Remember that it's a difficult skill to master, so keep up your daily PMR exercises. Rather than thinking of it as PMR (Progressive Muscle Relaxation), think of it as MRP – Muscle Relaxation Practice. You can do this (relax your reflex muscle) and repattern your lizard brain. The Neural Repatterning Technique (NRT) discussed in the next section can help you learn this skill because it uses a reduced intensity trigger, making it easier to relax.

Eight months after learning about muscle relaxation from the individual at the first misophonia conference, the same man reported his good news at the 2013 Misophonia Association Conference. After years of relaxing *after* being triggered to control his anger, he discovered that he could relax *before* triggers. As a member of the patient panel, he reported to the conference that he had virtually eliminated his misophonia by relaxing his muscles continually during trigger situations.[32] This is Applied Relaxation at its best! His initial physical reflex was pulling his shoulders toward his ears.

This likely worked at two levels. One, by relaxing before a trigger, he reduced the severity of the physical response to that trigger, and it created a lizard brain repatterning event so that the reflex was reduced ever so slightly for the next trigger. My journal article, "Treating the Initial Physical Reflex of Misophonia with the Neural Repatterning Technique: A Counterconditioning

Procedure," provides an extensive report of another individual who learned to relax her physical reflex. This article is available to you on MisophoniaTreatment.com. She started with PMR and then practiced relaxing to very small triggers during Neural Repatterning Technique (NRT) treatments using the Trigger Tamer app. After eliminating two triggers with the NRT treatment, she relaxed her muscles in real life situations, and continued to reduce her misophonic triggers.

It might sound trivial to learn to relax your muscles with PMR, but done properly, it can allow you to develop the skill you need to greatly reduce or overcome your misophonia.

Neural Repatterning Technique (NRT)

I developed the Neural Repatterning Technique in the spring of 2013. The treatment involves hearing an intermittent, very weak trigger while experiencing a positive situation, such as listening to your favorite music or talking about positive life experiences. The trigger is so weak that you don't have the negative emotions, so the treatment is a very positive experience. It proved to be successful that I decided to automate the treatment by creating a smartphone app available for iPhone and Android systems. The app is called the Misophonia Trigger Tamer. As a result, this treatment is often referred to as the Trigger Tamer treatment.

Martha's Story

Martha was a professional in her mid-forties with a lifelong history of misophonia ranging from mild to extremely debilitating. Efforts to decrease her symptoms included extensive work to reduce autonomic reactivity, which included breath work, relaxation techniques, noise reduction headsets, and musician plugs. She reduced her misophonia to the point that she rarely experienced extreme misophonic emotions, but she was still occasionally agitated by one trigger. After listening to a recording of the trigger in preparation for the NRT treatment, she reported that she became aware of the muscles behind the ear contracting when she heard the sound. She used the NRT treatment for the trigger stimulus and eliminated the reflex. With the reflex gone, the real-life trigger stimulus no longer elicited negative emotions.

Misophonia Response and NRT

When we think about misophonia, we generally think of it as having a trigger (a crunch sound) and that causes us to have an involuntary, extreme emotion or fight-or-flight response.

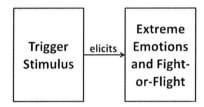

But misophonia is actually a two-step process. You hear the trigger, there is a physical reaction, a physical reflex, and the physical reflex jerks the extreme emotion or the fight-or-flight response out of you. If we can stop the physical reflex then there's no emotional response.

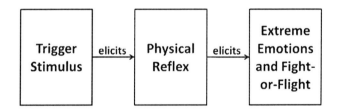

Therefore, the Neural Repatterning Technique is about stopping or reducing the emotional response to misophonia by first eliminating or reducing the physical misophonic reflex response. As shown below, the trigger stimulus causes a physical reflex in almost everyone with misophonia, and the physical reflex jerks the emotional response out of the person.

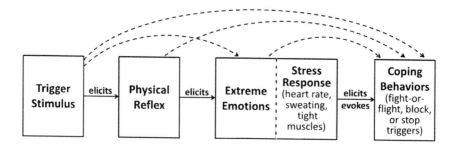

If we can eliminate the physical reflex, then it breaks the primary connection between the trigger and the emotions, as shown below.

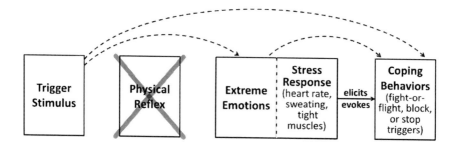

Usually the physical reflex is not completely eliminated with the NRT treatment. The reflex is greatly reduced, and it can die out with time, or may remain weak, providing a greatly reduced emotional response to the trigger.

Virginia's Story

This case is about eliminating a trigger to a family member singing around the house.

"I think probably it was about three weeks into it I started realizing that this is really working, because I have to say that I did not think anything would work. I think a lot of people feel that way who have this. And of course when I was young I felt that I was the only person in the world that had ever experienced this. But after about three weeks I started seeing the improvement, and it was gradual but it was definite. And I could tell that the trigger was going away, and it was getting lighter. And then when I started experiencing the trigger in real life and realized I wasn't having those emotions or that anger. It was like a miracle."

The Neural Repatterning Technique is not an unpleasant treatment. It is happy time. Virginia describes the Neural Repatterning Technique treatment sessions, using the Trigger Tamer app:

"I'm almost seventy-five years old, so for all of these years I have just tried to avoid these sounds. After I got through the apprehension of the whole thing, I began to look forward to this treatment and hearing those sounds was amazing to me. It was life changing."

Counterconditioning the Misophonia Reflex

As we discussed earlier in the book, there is something about experiencing a trigger that is causing the misophonia-conditioned reflex to be strengthened. It seems that the miso-emotions and tightened muscles after a trigger cause the reflex to become stronger.

To reduce the misophonia reflex, we need to hear a trigger and then have a *smaller* than typical reaction. We need to do something that will *reduce* or eliminate the miso-emotions, or have a situation where the reflex action (tight muscle) will be reduced or relax immediately after the trigger.

To get this effect, you could have positive emotions—relaxed or happy instead of the upset misophonia emotions. Another way would be to reduce the reflex using muscle relaxation, but you will need to relax *before* the trigger for this to work. For some reflexes, you can block the reflex with a more powerful reflex (this is rare, but tickling blocks a sexual arousal reflex and swallowing blocks or halts an esophagus constriction reflex). If the lizard brain is hearing the trigger (crunch) and sees a weaker reflex response a half a second after the trigger, then over time the lizard brain is going to reduce and even responding.

This is called *counterconditioning*. But the problem is that during the zero- to two-second pairing window after the trigger, the counterconditioning actions are not powerful enough to overcome the emotion that comes with misophonia. So it's very unusual that a person can just countercondition away one of these reflexes, although there are stories and cases where this has been done.

To overcome this limitation of counterconditioning, I started by reducing the trigger for the Neural Repatterning Technique. When we reduce the trigger enough, we diminish the intensity of the physical reflex. So instead of getting a full-sized reflex, you get a tiny reflex. It is like an allergy treatment for peanuts. If you are highly allergic to peanuts, you can die if you eat one. However, the allergy treatment consists of injecting you with a serum of the very thing that could be fatal. Only an infinitesimally small level is administered at any given time, which produces only a small response. By doing this multiple times, your body adjusts to the peanut and stops reacting. That's what the Neural Repatterning Technique is. You get just a little bit of the trigger sound to let your lizard brain stop responding.

It is usually best to use a recorded trigger, although I have worked with live triggers. When I was setting this up, I decided to use a rating scale of zero to five for the strength of the misophonia reflex, with five being a huge trigger and zero being something that doesn't cause a reaction or reflex.

What I look for with this Neural Repatterning Technique is to get a response of one. Maybe a two, but generally around a one, where the person can stay positive, calm, and happy. Then we pair the trigger with something that's pleasant. I have had it work with calming, relaxing music — something like pan-flute music, which you might hear if you get a massage. I have people who use happy, up-beat music. The first person I worked with liked a really harsh type of rock music. It was not my kind of music at all, but he really got into it. I also worked an individual where we talked during the treatment about uplifting, successful events in her life. That worked great for the positive stimulus. I have seen cases where the positive stimulus was massage. One person used pictures of her nephews, and another used pictures of her dog that she said just lifted her heart. But you need to have something that puts you in a positive state, either calm or happy, so that it can be paired against the disruptive response from the trigger, even though the response to the trigger is small. Once you determine what will put you in that positive state, then close your eyes, relax, and utilize the Trigger Tamer app so you have little reaction and allow your lizard brain to change.

Case Studies

The first person I ever did this with was a fifteen-year-old boy who triggered to family members, especially his mother crunching. We did this treatment with a live trigger, so his mom intermittently ate tiny pieces of Fritos while he listened to his favorite music. His reactions melted away. But then he went home and tried eating with his family, but couldn't because he still triggered to his mother's jaw movement. So they came back, and we did a couple of more treatments with the jaw movement, where he would look at his mother and then look away. Again, we kept the triggers small, and he would close his eyes or look away as soon as he felt the trigger, all the while he was listening to his music. Pretty soon he stopped triggering to his mother's jaw movement. He was marginally compliant with the assignments I gave him, but his misophonia reflex response changed very quickly. He went back to eating with his family again without disruption. It wasn't that it completely eliminated all of his misophonic reactions, but it brought them down to the level that it was reasonable and not emotionally upsetting.

The best-documented case I have was with a forty-eight year-old woman. This case is described in the journal article, "Counterconditioning Treatment for Misophonia," which is available on MisophoniaTreatment.com. She triggered to the sounds of her husband eating bread or sorbet and scratching his beard, and had a visual trigger to him putting his hand to his face. We used Skype for the treatment sessions. I had the triggers recorded so I could play them, and she would tell me the strength of the reflex response, whether that was a one or two or three. We worked on the trigger of her husband's eating bread for two weeks, and her response decreased dramatically. Then we took the second trigger, him eating sorbet, and her reflex response to it also dropped. Then we treated the trigger of the sound of him scratching of the beard, and it went down. Each of these triggers took two live treatment sessions with me, plus four homework sessions per week done independently. What we found was that her response to the eating bread trigger continued to die out in the real world, and completely went away. The last trigger we worked on was one of her husband putting his hand over his face. We found that when I put my hand to my face, it triggered her, so we worked with me as the trigger source. It took nine weeks to reduce her response to my hand movement. So her visual trigger was much more resistant to change than her sound triggers. When she finally was not triggered by me, she could generally ignore her husband's hand movement at home.

She and I both noticed a difference: her, at home and in life, and me, based on quantitative analysis. The graph shows her misophonia assessment questionnaire sum score. This is adding the value of each response of the twenty-one questions on the assessment. The sum score is a measure of the impact of misophonia on a person's life, or the general severity of their misophonia. The maximum sum score is sixty-three. She started at forty-one. After two treatments and the homework she was down to seventeen. This reduction was likely supported by improved management techniques I taught her in our first meeting. Two more treatments and the homework, and she was down to seven; but her husband had been out of town for a week, so that's artificially low because she had not heard her worst triggers. She was at a nine after two more weeks, and was still at nine after her eleventh session. We met four months after her treatment ended for a follow up assessment, and her sum score was only five. At the ten-month follow-up her sum score was only three.

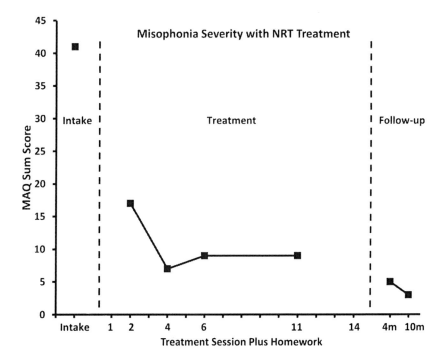

Although she still had triggers and occasionally needed to move away from a trigger situation, her response to triggers was small. She may notice a trigger and then look away, but it doesn't have the emotional upheaval. You can see from her overall misophonia sum score that she is not worried about misophonia. So that's really a very, very positive benefit to her life.

I worked with an eight-year-old and her parents. We did the Neural Repatterning Technique. Her counterconditioning stimulus was to dance around the room. The parents did multiple sessions with this little girl. They got rid of the trigger to one sound and then another, but they kept having some trouble at the table. Finally, they added some fan noise, and they eat together without a problem now. So while we saw improvement, this treatment didn't completely eliminate her misophonia.

I had a really interesting case where a college student was home for the summer.[33] She had a couple of really strong triggers with her mom. She did muscle relaxation training the first week before we started the NRT treatment. Her physical reflex was a hand clench, which is a pretty easy muscle to relax. Here's what she wrote on the Google Play App review: "My life is changed forever. I finally have control over my own suffering. Finding this app has been a complete miracle. Misophonia was ruining my life to the point where I couldn't stay in classes or couldn't concentrate because of the noises, and decided to go to Tom Dozier for help. After just two treatment sessions using the app, I could stand being around my mother while we ate (chewing and spoons on porcelain were some of my biggest triggers). Treatment for me worked very fast and I am excited to continue to eliminate other triggers. While I cannot completely eliminate reactions in real life, I barely react to the trigger. At least not with the rage I used to." (Congrats, Tom!!)

I talked to her after she went back to school, and she applied what she learned during the NRT treatment to real-life triggers. She found that she could ignore some triggers, especially when she relaxed her hands. Sometimes she needed to shake her hands a little when she was being triggered. She no longer experienced the overwhelming rage that she previously felt at school. I checked with her again at the end of the semester, which was six months after her treatment ended. Her misophonia severity was continuing to decline, both as rated by the overall severity and her response to individual triggers. Twelve months after her treatment, she was experiencing a slight increase in her overall misophonia severity, but her responses to the triggers we treated with NRT were completely gone. The increase in her twelve-month misophonia severity rating was likely due developing generalized anxiety disorder (GAD) between the six and twelve-month ratings. This is shown in the figure below. This case is also described in detail in my journal article, "Treating the Initial Physical Reflex of Misophonia with the Neural Repatterning Technique: A Counterconditioning Procedure," which is available on MisophoniaTreatment.com.

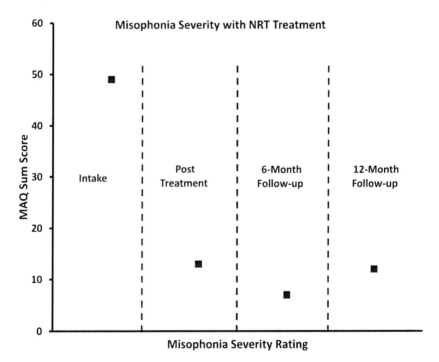

Another case is with one of the first people who bought the app. He called me and I helped him set up the app and get started with his treatment. Shortly thereafter, he sent me back this email. He wrote, "I have some excellent news. I've been doing my work with the app every day for about ten days, for at least an hour each session. If I'm feeling good I can do three hours or so while I'm at work. I was gradually increasing volume, frequency and length of the trigger sound (sniffling). Today I had a conversation with my roommate and partway through I realized he was sniffling and I was having no physical reflex. I then began focusing on the sound as if part of me knew something was supposed to happen but I had no negative feelings each time I heard the sound.

"I have been working on crunching, and I have definitely noticed a sensitivity decrease. I even have noticed an anxiety decrease when I know I might hear the trigger. I've realized I still really dislike the sound but I can handle it much better. Just the decrease in anxiety has been great."

The NRT treatment doesn't cure misophonia, but it can greatly reduce the reflex response. What do you need to do to make the Neural Repatterning Technique work for you? Your goal is to make your misophonia reflex response like an eye blink--a very small, non-upsetting response. But it needs to be a physical response. In addition to being a small reflex action, it needs to go away instantly.

The treatment seems to work better if the reflex is movement of a skeletal muscle, but this is not something you choose. Your misophonic reflex is what it is. It's already there. But if it's a skeletal muscle, then you can do muscle relaxation training so that you are better at relaxing that muscle before each trigger. You want the trigger rate (how often your hear a trigger) so triggers are being heard often enough that you have a lot of "learning" opportunities with the triggers, but you don't want it so much that it stresses you out.. Then you want to increase the length and the volume of the trigger as your reflex response goes down, so that you keep your physical response around a one on a scale of zero to five. I have seen cases where one hundred to three hundred exposures of a trigger produce a meaningful reduction in the reflex response with the Trigger Tamer.

Once the reflex goes away with one recorded trigger, then you switch to another, similar recording. When you stop responding to two to four examples of a single trigger with the Trigger Tamer, then you are ready for real-life triggers. You should still expect the reflex response to the trigger, but it will not be nearly as strong as it was before you did the Neural Repatterning Technique.

Generally I recommend you do the NRT treatment thirty minutes a day, four to six days a week. Most importantly, it needs to be a happy time. Smile. Enjoy the music. Relax. Do something fun and hear the tiny triggers. It's automated with the Trigger Tamer apps, so you can provide the treatment whenever and wherever you want. You have control of it, so you are the boss. You're in charge.

You need to make sure that you are actually experiencing the physical reflex. If you are just hearing a sound, and it is upsetting or disgusting, but there is no physical reflex, then the NRT treatment will not be effective. You also need to make sure that your lizard brain is changing during the treatment. If you do the treatment four to six times, and you don't need to increase the volume or duration of the trigger to keep your physical response at a level of "one," then your brain is not changing. This indicates there is some problem in the way the treatment is set up.

There are some conditions under which the Neural Repatterning Technique does not work. For example, if you can't be triggered by a sound or audiovisual recording, you can't use it. If you have no happy place or you can't relax, then it won't work for you. If the triggers linger once you are triggered—if the response doesn't go away instantly, then it won't work. An example of a lingering reflex response would be things like an intestine constriction, stomach constriction, or sexual arousal. Those tend to linger more, and they don't respond to the treatment because you can't get that small, brief response that ends instantly. However, I have seen it work with nausea. A person said their stomach flipped and it worked for her.

The Neural Repatterning Technique is suitable for specific triggers, where you have a stimulus of a single person or single thing, or for an emerging trigger—one that's just coming on. An emerging trigger will almost always be a single-person, single-place situation. NRT is not suitable for a general trigger, something like gum chewing or sniffling by anyone, anywhere, but it can be used for a general trigger to practice Applied Relaxation so that you can relax when triggered in real-life or for a single situation. For example, if you trigger to sniffling everywhere, you can use NRT for the trigger of your child sniffling.

I had one of my best students with this treatment try to overcome a general sniffing trigger. She was a teacher, and she did the homework faithfully. She did the muscle relaxation regularly, and she didn't trigger with the app. But when she was in her classroom at school and a kid sniffed, she still triggered. The problem was that the setting for the NRT training and the real-life trigger were very different. The research shows that conditioned reflexes can be very context- or situation-sensitive.

The Trigger Tamer Apps

There are two versions of the Trigger Tamer apps. The app with the blue brain icon is called the Misophonia Trigger Tamer,

 and it uses an audio recording for the trigger. The app with the green head is the Visual Trigger Tamer, and it uses a video recording for the trigger.

MisophoniaTrigger Tamer, Home Screen

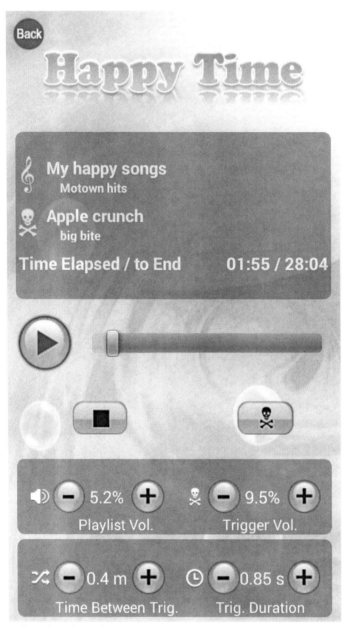

Misophonia Trigger Tamer, Treatment Screen

116

Visual Trigger Tamer, Home Screen

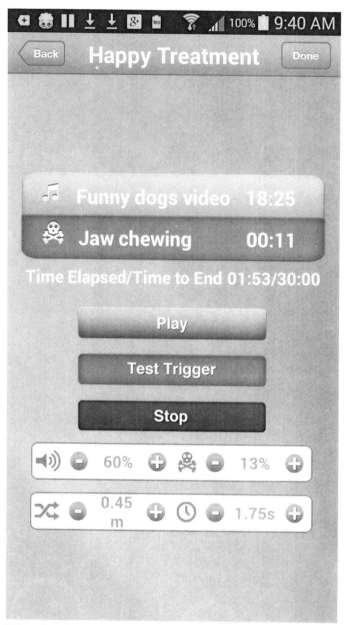

Visual Trigger Tamer, Treatment Control Screen

The Misophonia Trigger Tamer has better control of the trigger for sounds and is available on both iTunes and Google Play. The Visual Trigger Tamer is released to Google Play and the iTunes version is in development. It allows you to use a visual and audio trigger, so if you have trouble triggering to an audio recording, you may trigger to the video/audio combination. But the Visual Trigger Tamer has less control of the timing and options for the trigger. The Misophonia Trigger Tamer has a recorder and good sound editor built into it, but for the Visual Trigger Tamer, you will need to use other programs to record and edit your triggers.

Another difference in the two apps is that the Misophonia Trigger Tamer only allows audio recordings for the positive stimulus playlist, but the Visual Trigger Tamer lets you use a combination of audio recordings, pictures, and videos for the positive stimulus playlist.

The Neural Repatterning Technique complements other treatments such as the Misophonia Management Protocol, where you use either background sound or the audiologist-provided sound generators that go behind the ear. The MMP provides a way to reduce your real-world response to triggers, and the NRT treatment helps you bring those reflexes down to make it even better. Cognitive or dialectal behavioral therapy (CBT or DBT) are very good for dealing with the emotional upheaval from the trigger, but they don't get rid of the actual trigger response. Adding the NRT treatment helps you reduce the misophonia trigger reflex that is the cause of the strong misophonic emotions.

Hypnotherapy - SRT

Until Chris Pearson developed the Sequent Repatterning Therapy for misophonia, hypnotherapy had been broadly ineffective or had provided only short-term relief. Misophonia has generally been treated as a phobia by hypnotherapists. Because of the physical reflex of misophonia, it has been impossible for individuals with misophonia to ignore or not respond to trigger stimuli. Actually, as discussed earlier, the misophonic person is responding to the combination of the sound and the physical sensation caused by the physical reflex. We can ignore sounds, but we cannot ignore the physical jolt or sensation of the reflex.

Sequent Repattering Therapy (SRT) is generally effective because it allows a person to feel the physical sensation of the misophonic reflex while *not* having the emotional response. The context of a physical sensation can have a great effect on the emotional response. If a nurse in the doctor's office sticks you with a needle, you can stay completely calm. But if a person walks up to you and sticks you with a straight pin, then we can almost guarantee that you will have a strong emotional response. SRT builds a strong calming response over a series of sessions and then teaches the patient to respond to the physical sensation with the calming response rather than anger. As shown below, SRT disconnects the emotional response from the physical reflex.

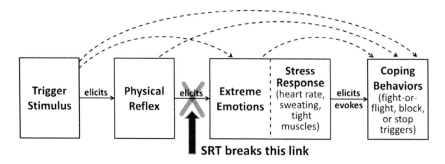

The SRT treatment is a series of five treatment steps that usually require up to eight hypnotherapy sessions. Steps one, two, and three build the emotional stability and strength of the individual, and develops a calm reflex. Step four disconnects the emotional misophonic response from the physical reflex and replaces it with the calm reflex. Because almost all misophonic individuals have the same physical reflex for all of their triggers, this step reduces the emotional response for all triggers. Step five of the process works to disconnect the physical reflex from the trigger stimulus. This step requires addressing each trigger individually.

In 2013, Chris Pearson treated fifteen patients using SRT. Patients reported their misophonia severity score from one to ten as a "Subjective Units of Distress" (SUD), with one being non-existent to ten being very severe. Nine had a large reduction in the severity of their misophonia; rating one to three after treatment. Four patients had moderate improvement, with a SUD rating of four to six after treatment (and at least a three point reduction). One person dropped out of treatment and another did not respond to the treatment. In May, 2015, follow-up data was obtained on eleven of the thirteen individuals who responded to treatment. Of these, six had maintained their improvement, four had a decline but still had meaningful improvement, and one with moderate improvement had relapsed. Each had been asked to perform a daily calming exercise several times a day, which took less than a minute each time. Of those doing the daily calming exercise, five of six were maintaining the improvement and one had a decline in improvement.

A major effort is underway by Chris Pearson and the Misophonia Treatment Institute to develop an SRT training program for hypnotherapists so this treatment can be more widely available. As of this writing, we have trained our first SRT hypnotherapists. SRT treatment can be provided by internet video-chat, so SRT is an option for anyone with a good internet connection. We are at an early phase of developing this treatment, but the results of the individuals treated in 2013 make us hopeful that this treatment may provide meaningful improvement to many individuals with misophonia. So far we have not identified any limitations for the applicability of SRT hypnotherapy treatment for misophonia. It has been used to successfully treat individuals as young as ten years of age.

Successful SRT treatment can be accomplished by completing the first four of five steps. This disconnects the miso-emotional response from the physical reflex. A small percentage of individuals respond to the final step of SRT treatment and actually

121

stop having the physical reflex response to triggers. Still, reducing the misophonic severity from moderate to mild or severe to mild is a significant positive benefit for anyone with misophonia.

I believe that we can accomplish even further improvement by combining the SRT treatment with other treatment techniques, such as the Neural Repatterning Technique or muscle relaxation, which work to reduce the physical reflex response to triggers.

Psychosomatic Remediation Technique (PRT)

It was mid-October, 2013. I had determined that many people had a physical reflex to trigger sounds, and that the actual reflex varied. I was providing free NRT treatment for a patient as part of my investigation of misophonia, and this particular patient's reflex was a stomach constriction. This was a difficult reflex to address with the NRT treatment because the constriction seemed to linger after the tiny trigger, and a person cannot willfully relax their stomach. I was searching for a way to reduce or halt the stomach constriction, but was unable to find anything. So I called my good friend, Scott Sessions, who is a chiropractor and a holistic treatment provider in rural Wyoming. About ten years earlier, Dr. Sessions had cured my anaphylactic reaction to shrimp by stimulating specific meridian points. I thought that maybe he had an idea of how to stop a stomach constriction reflex. We discussed misophonia and he informed me of a fortuitous event —he and his son would soon be returning to my hometown. He said he would come to my home while in the area to show me what he could do. Little did I know that he was thinking, "I haven't considered treating misophonia before, but I have an idea worth investigating." My request for help turned out to be the catalyst for the PRT protocol that he has since developed and continues to refine.

My daughter and granddaughter, who had misophonia, were here when Dr. Sessions arrived, so he used them to show me what he could do to address an unwanted reflex. He could not stop a reflex once it started, but he thought he might be able to prevent the reflex from occurring. I watched as he worked on my granddaughter. After fifteen minutes of questions, acupressure, and a little spinal manipulation, my granddaughter no longer triggered to her arch trigger-nemesis: her brother. My daughter asked Dr. Sessions to treat her. After another fifteen minutes, she no longer triggered to any of her triggers. If I had not seen it, I would not have believed it. But I am open enough to believe that there are things that I do not understand (like how Dr. Sessions cured me of my allergies). We were ecstatic.

Over the next few months, Dr. Sessions treated a few more individuals with misophonia with mixed, but mostly positive, results. Most responded; some did not. One impediment to progress on this treatment technique was Dr. Sessions' remote location in Thayne, Wyoming, or as he calls it, "the middle of nowhere." In March 2014, my daughter and granddaughter had been trigger free for over four months. We wanted to be certain that these results would be typical, and we felt the best way to do that was hold a treatment seminar in an easily accessible location. In April, we held a treatment seminar in Anaheim, CA. The PRT protocol at that time required about thirty minutes to complete. At that seminar, we treated thirty-one individuals. About a quarter had complete elimination of their misophonic triggers. Another quarter had a large reduction in their misophonic symptoms, and half had no change at all. These were not the numbers we were anticipating based on the previous patients treated. Additionally, the improvement generally declined with time for the group that responded. Because Dr. Sessions' practice was in Thayne, it was difficult for individuals to visit him for follow-up treatments.

I asked my daughter why she thought she and her daughter had sustained positive results. (As of the writing of this book, she still is trigger free and her daughter has developed only one trigger, which very rarely occurs, so she is essentially trigger free). She said that she made a concerted effort to keep herself and her daughter away from stressful situations where there were trigger sounds. About three months after treatment, my daughter had a very bad trigger experience. She was stressed-out, hungry, tired, and sick. The trigger hit her full force. She avoided the trigger for a few days. She had another mild response to that trigger, but none since then.

Because the results were not lasting for most patients, we decided to stop promoting the treatment. Fortunately, Dr. Sessions is passionate about helping people and continued to work hard over the next year at developing the PRT protocol. As of this writing, the treatment protocol has expanded and now takes twenty hours spread over a six-day period. Results are again promising. He is seeing over fifty percent-sustained success with the treatment. I say, "Go, Scott. Go!"

At this time, if you want the PRT treatment, you will need to visit Dr. Sessions in Thayne, Wyoming. Thayne is about an hour south of Jackson, Wyoming in beautiful Star Valley. You will need to be there for a week. You also need to be able to return for a second treatment if your treatment results are not sustained. For more information on PRT, go to dayspringhealth.com or MisophoniaTreatment.com.

CBT/DBT

Cognitive behavioral therapy (CBT) focuses on a person's thoughts, feelings, and behaviors to identify unhealthy patterns. The patient and therapist then develop appropriate healthy patterns of thoughts, feelings and behaviors to replace the unhealthy patterns. Dialectical behavior therapy is a form of CBT that puts a specific focus on a person's arousal response to certain emotional situations.

A case study of cognitive behavioral therapy (CBT) to treat misophonia in a young woman reported elimination of impaired social functioning at end of treatment and at four-months post-treatment, although the woman still found the trigger stimuli unpleasant.[34] The treatment plan included "(a) a cognitive component to challenge dysfunctional automatic thoughts, (b) a behavioral component to interrupt maladaptive and avoidant coping strategies and practice helpful ones, and (c) a physiological component to help recalibrate her autonomic reactivity." This last component was thirty minutes of exercise a day, and it was unclear whether the patient did this or not. It seems as if the individual still did not like the sounds because she was still triggering to them, as this treatment did not address the physical reflex. But if the individual could remain calm, then perhaps with time the physical reflex would decline. This needs more research.

A second case study was reported on CBT treatment for two youths with misophonia ages eleven and seventeen.[35] I preface the description of treatment by saying that I do not advise this method because it used enticing rewards to motivate a child to control or suppress her outward, aggressive coping behavior after a trigger, without reducing the physical reflex. This has created situations where a child controlled their "acting out" to triggers, but inwardly developed new triggers and stronger misophonic reflexes until the misophonia re-emerged much worse than when the treatment began. The treatment in this study included psychoeducation about misophonia and focused on helping the patients develop the ability to tolerate triggers without aggressive or avoidant behaviors. The treatment included a progressive exposure of trigger severity and response prevention. This allowed the patients to develop the ability to tolerate the triggers and remain calm. A reward hierarchy was provided for the younger patient for completion of the exposure steps. Cognitive restructuring was included to address dysfunctional beliefs about the sounds, such as "my family makes these sounds to annoy/aggravate me." Both youth progressed though treatment and were able to eat with their families without accommodations. Both youth showed a reduction of their misophonia severity at the end of treatment based on a self-report questionnaire, though the decline for the younger child was fairly small. The study did not include any follow-up measures for the youth.

My concern about this treatment is that it did not address the initial physical reflex. It was successful at helping the youth develop the emotional and behavioral control to stay calm when triggered, but without eliminating the aversive reflex, there is a risk that the conditioned physical reflex will strengthen and other triggers will develop. It is very beneficial for a person with misophonia to learn to remain calm when triggered, but this does not eliminate the risk of an escalation of misophonia severity through repeated exposure to triggers. The risks here are discussed more fully in the chapter How Triggers Spread.

CBT can be helpful reducing the emotional upheaval that comes with misophonia, and there many are anecdotal reports of individuals benefiting from this form of treatment. CBT or similar therapy is also recommended by the Misophonia Management Protocol to help a person change the way they think about triggers and live with misophonia as a chronic condition.

Neurofeedback

There is no definitive data or published case studies on the effectiveness of neurofeedback, but there are some highly discussed success stories. For every success story, there are many other reports of individuals where neurofeedback had no effect on their misophonia. Dr. Randall Lyle of Cedar Rapids, Iowa has several cases of very significant reduction in misophonic symptoms, and he is a highly skilled neurofeedback practitioner. These cases generally require anywhere from 40-100, or even more, neurofeedback sessions, so it is a slow brain-change process.

Because this is a slow process, it seems possible that neurofeedback may actually address misophonia indirectly.

Neurofeedback is widely reported to improve many conditions that would improve general health and wellbeing. Dr. Lyle writes that neurofeedback can facilitate healing of depression, anxiety, stress, chronic fatigue, pain, migraines, posttraumatic stress disorder (PTSD), obsessive thoughts, and compulsions.[36] Reducing any of these conditions would likely improve general wellness, and improved wellness is associated with reduction in misophonic symptoms.

Considering the multiple-step view of misophonia presented previously, if neurofeedback makes a person less reactive to aversive stimuli, then the first effect would be to reduce the emotional response. This could allow a weakening of the conditioned misophonic physical reflex, which seems to be strengthened because of the overall misophonic response to triggers (and the repeated occurrence of triggers). I mentioned Connor, the Marine with PTSD, who developed misophonia in Afghanistan. He virtually eliminated his misophonia by practicing progressive muscle relaxation and responding to triggers with "no threat, but thank you." The muscle relaxation improved his sleep and reduced his PTSD symptoms. The improved wellness was likely a large factor in this immediate reduction in misophonia, and the sustained, low emotion responses could have allowed his conditioned misophonia reflex to continually weaken and extinguish (go away completely).

The bottom line is that neurofeedback has been demonstrated to improve a person's health and wellbeing, so this treatment could be very beneficial to you if you have general health problems, and resolving health problems would likely reduce your misophonia symptoms.

Medication for Anxiety or Depression

In a study I conducted, we collected individual treatment histories and their overall effect on misophonia. Because participants reported multiple treatments and only the overall effect, the effect of a single treatment method is somewhat disguised. A regression analysis of the data indicated that, on average, taking medication to treat anxiety or depression had a measurable positive effect on misophonia severity. I am not suggesting this is for everyone, but if you have a problem with depression or anxiety that is unrelated to misophonia, appropriate medication for that condition could also reduce your misophonia symptoms because it could improve your overall health and wellbeing. Again, it is likely that this medication does not directly address the misophonia, but has an indirect, positive effect on it.

Tinnitus Retraining Therapy

Drs. Pawel and Margaret Jastreboff reported using Tinnitus Retraining Therapy (TRT) to provide treatment for misophonia.[37] There are many audiologists trained in TRT. Some only treat tinnitus and hyperacusis and some also treat misophonia. TRT uses positive sound protocols, noise generators, and counseling. This is similar to the Misophonia Management Protocol (MMP), except the MMP does not use the positive sound protocols. A journal article reported the treatment of 184 individuals with misophonia. Of this group, 152 individuals (83%) "showed significant improvement." *Significant improvement* was defined as at least a two-point reduction on a zero to ten scale to the question, "How much of a problem is your misophonia?" Based on the data reported, I cannot tell if this treatment is more effective than the Misophonia Management Protocol reviewed in the previous chapter. There is a well-established issue with self-report data of this type, especially when the change reported is small. Patients are unconsciously influenced to give answers that are expected, so if a patient wants to get better and the doctor wants them to get better, this can influence the patient's answer.[38] This same bias exists with my patients or anyone's patients, but it is a larger issue when the change due to treatment is small. Nevertheless, it is hopeful that the treatment had a positive effect on many of the individuals, and I look forward to further information about the effectiveness of TRT treatment and the benefits of the individual components.

Blocking a Reflex

There are a few reflexes that you can block. For example, if you are having esophagus constriction, you can swallow to stop that reflex. You may be able to block a sexual arousal reflex with someone tickling you or a deep yoga stretch.

One misophonic reflex that I have seen several times is a gasp —a quick breath. If you have this reflex, then you may be very lucky. You can overpower your miso-reflex by breathing. Just don't hold your breath. I call this scuba breathing (yes, underwater diving). When I took scuba lessons, they taught us that we had to always be breathing in or out. We never held our breath, because to do so could cause our lungs to explode. So if you have a gasp reflex, just practice scuba breathing. Breathe in slowly for four to five seconds, then breathe out at the same rate. By willfully controlling your breathing muscles, you will greatly reduce your misophonia.

If you discover a way to block a reflex, let me know so we can share your success. It may be possible to use Botox or some other medical treatment to block a physical reflex. This could be a good research study.

16. Treatments to Avoid

As discussed previously, there is something about the misophonia reflex response to triggers that causes them to strengthen with repeated exposure. A commonly occurring view of misophonia is that it sounds a lot like obsessive-compulsive disorder (OCD) or a phobia so it makes sense to someone who does not understand the different components of the misophonic response to treat misophonia the same way that you would treat OCD or a phobia. To treat a person with OCD, a person is allowed to engage in the compulsive behavior, but after they do it, they must repeat it many times or do some other thing that takes time and effort. This establishes a form of punishment or a price for doing the compulsive behavior so the person will resist the compulsion to avoid the extra work.

This makes no sense for misophonia, because the misophonic physical reflex response is an involuntary behavior, and so is the emotional response. If the punishment is applied for a person getting angry, it will simply increase the frustration because the person is trying to not get angry already, but cannot stay calm. If the punishment is applied for acting out (coping behaviors) after the physical reflex and emotional response, then we are trying to change the acting out behavior using punishment. Using punishment almost always includes bad feelings of some sort, and so it is far less likely to work than using a positive reward for controlling antisocial coping behaviors.

In either case, controlling the coping behaviors does not address the first four components of the misophonic response, and so repeated exposure to the trigger will simply cause these responses to become stronger.

Traditional exposure therapy is probably the worst possible treatment for misophonia. There are some reports of this working for people, but I expect it will only work when a person is very motivated to engage in this treatment. It is definitely a treatment that should be avoided for children. With exposure therapy, the individual is exposed to full strength, real-life triggers for a period of time. This may initially be a short time, and then be progressively longer and longer. The problem with this treatment is that it actually strengthens the initial physical reflex and the emotional response during the treatment. It can also lead to new triggers developing during this process.

There are many reports of individuals on misophonia groups who say that such exposure therapy made their misophonia worse. Occasionally there is a person who says they did exposure therapy and had great improvement. So beware of exposing yourself to full strength triggers as a way of reducing your misophonia. You will likely be asked to listen to some triggers with CBT, but you will also be taught ways to calm yourself. It is okay to practice this with a few triggers, and then slowly build up the skill of relaxing, which is a way of reducing the emotional response to the triggers. If someone suggests you try traditional exposure therapy, especially someone who is not an expert on misophonia, I suggest you consider another treatment or even another treatment provider.

17. Misophonia and Children

This chapter reflects my experience with a number of children I have worked with and the comments of parents and adults with misophonia.

As we already discussed, misophonia develops through an experience process called "conditioning." It is a process where we develop or acquire a reflex reaction to some predictable or repeating stimulus. It is an automatic human process, and we cannot "make" a child do it or not do it. The process consists of pairing a stimulus with an emotional and physical condition. The stimulus can be any repeating sound. The most common one is an eating sound, but it could also be a breathing sound, muffled voices through walls, typing, a consonant sound of your voice (like "s"), or any other sound.

In an article about treating misophonia and other hearing conditions, Dr. Pawel and Margaret Jastreboff wrote that misophonia reactions "are governed by the principles of conditioned reflexes, with the subconscious part of the brain playing a significant role." (In 2002, the Jastreboffs proposed the name "misophonia" for this condition.) This view of misophonia was also supported in a study that developed a diagnostic criteria for misophonia.[39] I include this as support for the idea that misophonia is developed through experience, and not something that just happens because of a brain defect or genetic condition as some suppose.[40] However, genetics often play a role in setting the stage for a child to develop misophonia. In the following pages, I talk about Type 1, Type 2, and SPD children. Whether a child is any of these is probably mostly influenced by their genetics.

Two Types of Kids Develop Misophonia

I have generally found that there are two types of children who develop misophonia.

"Type 1" Kids: First, there is the compliant and sensitive child. This child is cooperative, caring, and emotionally in tune with the feelings of others. The child may not show any outward signs of being upset, but when mommy or daddy is agitated, they become upset, which is manifests itself by tightening certain muscles (the specific muscle varies from one child to the next). Any repeated physical action that accompanies the distress can become a trigger if there is a sound that increases the distress, such as lip smacking that had been identified as completely unacceptable by a parent.

After a Type 1 child develops misophonia, the child may become very demanding regarding the trigger and have emotional outbursts. This is a common characteristic of everyone with misophonia (adults and children alike). It does not make him a Type 2 kid.

"Type 2" Kids: The second type of child to develop misophonia is strong-willed, volatile, and has a strong sense of fairness (though likely incorrect). This child creates her own world of distress. She may complain about bedtime, leaving the park, having to turn off the video game, or not getting to do something. This child will often have conflict with a parent or sibling.

A ten-year-old girl I worked with developed her misophonia trigger to her younger brother's crunching at the dinner table. They had a running battle of "stop staring at me." She would get upset and yell, while he would argue and crunch, crunch, crunch, displaying open-mouth eating because he had a stopped-up nose. After the reflex developed, when she heard him crunch his food, her brain automatically caused the state of distress that she had when fighting with him at the dinner table.

On a Facebook group post, I posed the following question.

"I have observed that kids with miso generally fall into two classes.

133

"#1. Well behaved, almost ideal kids. Very conscientious and cooperative. Seemingly stable emotionally.

"#2. Strong-willed kids, who get upset easily, and make strong, emotional demands for what they want.

"Would you say that your child fits #1, #2, or other (please specify)?"

I got thirty-six responses. Twenty-one for #1, and thirteen for #2. Two responses were for both. I think this is pretty good agreement with my general observation.

Developing the First Misophonia Trigger

The reason that these two types of kids develop misophonia is because both types experience emotional distress. The Type 1 kids may have distress from being sensitive to the feelings of others. It is my guess that kids with anxiety or obsessive-compulsive disorder are Type 1 kids, and these genetic conditions also create distress that could lead to misophonia. Type 2 kids create their own emotional upheaval and distress. Either way, it's the pairing of a distressed state and a repeating sound, especially when the repeating sound plays a part in the distress of the individual.

Is Misophonia Caused by Genetics or Environment (Experience)?

The answer is "both." I have four children. The first and the last seemed to be cast from the same mold. They were very much Type 2 children. The other two children were very unique and different. One was a Type 1, and the other was neither a Type 1 nor a Type 2. My daughter with misophonia was a Type 2. Her brother, who had a very similar disposition, does not have misophonia.

Genetics plays a large part in a child being a Type 1 or a Type 2, but experience in the home also plays a critical part. Some kids are extremely mellow. This has both a genetic component and an experience component. These mellow kids seem very unlikely to develop misophonia. We should not say that misophonia is caused by genetics or by environment: it takes both. What we can say is that misophonia is not simply a genetic condition that turns on like a switch at a certain age.

"Type SPD" Kids: Sensory Processing Disorder or Sensory Over-Responsiveness. There does seem to be a third group, which could either be Type 1 or Type 2 kids (or neither). These are kids who have sensory sensitivities. With these kids, sounds are more upsetting. Clothing tags, clothes, shoes, or light may cause distress. These kids simply have more times when they are distressed with a connection to repeating sounds. This also seems to contribute to development of misophonia, and was pointed out in one research study.[41] But SPD is primarily a genetic, inborn condition and it is a distinct condition. Although the symptoms of SPD and misophonia are often similar, misophonia is not a form of SPD, and SPD is not a form of misophonia.

What's a Parent to Do?

This is a difficult situation for you as a parent. Others (or you) may say that your child is behaving like a brat. It seems that your child should be able to just ignore the sound, but they don't! Maybe you think your child just wants to have power over the family. Misophonia is a unique disorder where a common sound causes your child great distress. Your child is not choosing to be bothered by the sound—being distressed by the sound is an involuntary, reflex reaction.

Here are some things that the misophonia response is not (I'm saying this specifically to the parents, but also to the spouses and close friends). Misophonia is not a way to control you as the parent or others. It's not a way to get attention. It's not a choice. This is a reflex reaction. And it's not something that the person is going to just get used to. It's very aversive, and it's very difficult to deal with.

There's a coping response, and that's what the person does in response to being triggered. They may cover their ears. They may run away. They may push or shove, and this is really also jerked out of the person who is being assaulted, because misophonia is this kind of assault on the body and the mind. This is automatic, somewhat like an automatic response of fight-or-flight.

It varies with each person and sometimes it's perplexing to the parents. Your child can have a friend over to your house and the friend or you crunch a chip, and your child doesn't explode. But when there are no friends at the house and you crunch a chip the child goes ballistic. Now it doesn't mean that the child wasn't triggered when their friend was there. They were still zapped. But responding and acting out would be too costly; it could be too embarrassing to them. It could cause them to be ostracized from their friends. Please note that just because a child doesn't act out in that situation, it doesn't mean that they weren't triggered and they didn't feel it. A person may be irritated in one setting and yell, but if they were stopped by police they would be irritated, but wouldn't yell in that situation.

If you try to let misophonia "run its natural course," you should expect it to get progressively worse with time. More trigger sounds will develop. Visual triggers will develop. Triggers often develop at school or with friends. Once this happens, misophonia can have a large, negative impact on your child's life. It can be debilitating. The most important thing that you can do for your child with misophonia is to implement an extensive management plan so your child is triggered as little as possible. In fact, there should not be situations where the child has to endure triggers. Work out a family plan and be diligent at following it. If you do this, you can slow or prevent the increase of the number of triggers and the severity of misophonic responses. In many cases, this is the best thing you can do, especially when your child is very young

Carefully consider your treatment options. They are generally expensive and not covered by insurance. Some are difficult and time consuming to implement. No treatment works for every child. But there is hope because we are making steady progress on misophonia treatment, and more researchers are getting involved.

18. Misophonia or Conditioned Aversive Reflex Disorder (CARD)

While the term "misophonia" is commonly used for this condition and has a catchy ring to it, in the course of my experience and research I have concluded it does not accurately describe this disorder.

Firstly, "misophonia" —literally, a hatred or dislike of sound—only refers to the emotional response to auditory triggers. Many individuals have visual triggers, and there are anecdotal reports of olfactory (smell) and tactile (touch) triggers. It has been proposed that an extreme emotional response to visual triggers be named misokinesia,[42] which would be a second name for the same phenomenon.

Secondly, the term "misophonia" puts the focus on the individual's experience of a strong dislike of sound. Liking or hating something is generally an evaluative process that can be altered by thoughtful consideration, but this is generally not the case with this condition. You can hate punk rock, but that's not the same thing as having an involuntary physical response to it.

Finally, a disorder that is fundamentally an emotional response places the neurological emphasis on the limbic system, while a disorder that is fundamentally a conditioned reflex response places the neurological emphasis on the autonomic nervous system. Misophonia is a conditioned reflex response. This distinction has important implications for both research and the development of treatments. Therefore, the term "misophonia" does not clearly indicate the reflexive nature of the condition, which can also be a source of misunderstanding when communicating to family members, teachers, coworkers, and employers.

I propose that Conditioned Aversive Reflex Disorder (CARD) is a more descriptive and appropriate name for this condition. It could also be called Aversive Reflex Disorder (ARD). This name puts the focus on the reflex nature of the disorder and on the etiology of the reflex, which is classical conditioning. CARD easily incorporates all modalities of trigger stimuli. Specifying it as a disorder requires a diagnostic criteria to determine a clinical level versus subclinical level of such reflexes. This disorder presents with great variety of aversive reflexes, where one person may have a single aversive reflex, as illustrated previously in the case of Paul (the middle aged adult with only a trigger to a ringtone)), while another individual may suffer a debilitating condition that causes them to be unable to tolerate a typical work environment.

I had one patient whose primary emotional response to the trigger was fear. She had typical misophonic anticipatory anxiety of being triggered, but felt no fear when discussing the trigger stimuli. She had many of the common misophonic triggers, such as sniffing, gum chewing, breathing, and coughing. Was this phonophobia (fear of the sound)? No. It was CARD. Her physical reflex was a gasp. When she heard the trigger stimulus, she gasped, which jerked her body. She was easily startled, and the involuntary jerk of her muscles startled her, causing the fear emotions. Clearly this was a conditioned aversive reflex for her. The diagnosis of misophonia is confusing, but she clearly fits the description for CARD.

There are other disorders that have similar symptoms to CARD but appear more strongly influenced by genetics, such as sensory processing disorder or being a highly sensitive person. . These are likely cause by inborn, genetic conditions rather that an acquired reflex as CARD, and CARD rather than misophonia, makes this distinction clear.

Additionally, the name CARD immediately helps others understand that this is a real condition which happens to a person rather than the person being overly emotional to something "they should just ignore."

Your Next Step

Thank you for reading this book. For more information, go to the Misophonia Treatment Institute website at MisophoniaTreatment.com. The Misophonia Treatment Institute is committed to increasing misophonia awareness, providing helpful information, and developing and disseminating misophonia treatments. There is a list of treatment providers that is ever-increasing. For some treatments, you will need to find someone in your area, but others can be accessed using internet video-chat, so help is available, regardless of where you live.

I hope this book has increased your understanding of misophonia (or CARD). But more so, I hope that you will take the ideas, tricks, treatments, and techniques described herein and take action to improve your life or the life of someone close to you. Overcoming misophonia is a process, not a single action. It may take sustained, consistent work, such as doing Progressive Muscle Relaxation every day. Developing misophonia, including all the variations of triggers, has probably taken many years. Overcoming misophonia is also a process, where you gradually reduce your response to triggers and allow your lizard brain to learn a new way to respond to them.

There is hope for you to overcome your misophonia. I also have great hope that with a proper understanding of misophonia, many other professionals and researchers will determine new ways that will help you reduce and even eliminate your misophonia reflexes.

I wish you well!

References

Berkowitz, L. (1983). Aversively stimulated aggression: Some parallels and differences in research with animals and humans. *American Psychologist, 38*(11), 1135-1144. doi:10.1037/0003-066X.38.11.1135

Berkowitz, L., Cochran, S. T., & Embree, M. C. (1981). Physical pain and the goal of aversively stimulated aggression. *Journal of Personality and Social Psychology, 40*(4), 687 -700. doi:10.1037/0022-3514.40.4.687

Bernstein, R. E., Angell, K. L., & Dehle, C. M. (2013). A brief course of cognitive behavioural therapy for the treatment of misophonia: A case example. *The Cognitive Behaviour Therapist, 6*(10), 1-13. doi:10.1017/S1754470X13000172

Borkovec, T. D., & Sides, J. K. (1979). Critical procedural variables related to the physiological effects of progressive relaxation: A review. *Behaviour Research and Therapy, 17*(2), 119-125. doi:10.1016/0005-7967(79)90020-2

Bourne, E. J. (2011). *The anxiety and phobia workbook.* Oakland, CA: New Harbinger Publications.

Conrad, A., & Roth, W. T. (2007). Muscle relaxation therapy for anxiety disorders: It works but how?. *Journal of Anxiety Disorders, 21*(3), 243-264. doi:10.1016/j.janxdis.2006.08.001

Dehghan-Nayeri, N., & Adib-Hajbaghery, M. (2011). Effects of progressive relaxation on anxiety and quality of life in female students: A non-randomized controlled trial. *Complementary Therapies in Medicine, 19*(4), 194-200. doi: 10.1016/j.ctim.2011.06.002

Donahoe, J. W., & Vegas, R. (2004). Pavlovian conditioning: The CS-UR relation. *Journal Of Experimental Psychology: Animal Behavior Processes, 30*(1), 17-33. doi:10.1037/0097-7403.30.1.17

Dozier, T. H. (2014, February). *Misophonia: An aversive conditioned reflex to soft sounds*. Poster presented at the annual convention of the California Association for Behavior Analysis, San Francisco, CA. Available from: http://misophoniatreatment.com/wp-content/uploads/2014/03/Misophonia-as-a-conditioned-reflex-2014-CalABA.pdf

Dozier, T. H. (2015a). Counterconditioning treatment for misophonia. *Clinical Case Studies*. Published online before print January 20, 2015. doi: 10.1177/1534650114566924

Dozier, T. H. (2015b). Etiology, composition, development and maintenance of misophonia: A conditioned aversive reflex disorder. *Psychological Thought, 8*(1), 114–129, doi:10.5964/psyct.v8i1.132

Dozier, T. H. (in press). Treating the initial physical reflex of misophonia with the neural repatterning technique: A counterconditioning procedure. *Psychological Thought*

Edelstein, M., Brang, D., Rouw, R., & Ramachandran, V.S. (2013). Misophonia: Physiological investigations and case descriptions. *Frontiers in Human Neuroscience, 7*(296), 1-11. doi: 10.3389/fnhum.2013.00296

Fayzullina, S., Smith, R. P., Furlotte, N., Hu, Y., Hinds, D., & Tung, J. Y. (2015). *Genetic associations with traits in 23andMe customers*. Retrieved from http://blog.23andme.com/wp-content/uploads/2015/03/5-N8XiOLkGIgydwX_SS-IQ_23-08_Genetic_Associations_With_Traits1.pdf on July 3, 2015.

Furedy, J. J., & Riley, D. M. (1987). Human Pavlovian autonomic conditioning and the cognitive paradigm. In G. Gavey (Ed.) *Cognitive processes and Pavlovian conditioning in humans* (pp. 1-25). Chichester, West Sussex, UK: John Wiley & Sons Ltd.

Goubet, N., Strasbaugh, K., & Chesney, J. (2007). Familiarity breeds content? Soothing effect of a familiar odor on full-term newborns. *Journal of Developmental & Behavioral Pediatrics* 28(3), 189-194. doi:10.1097/dbp.0b013e31802d0b8d

Howard, G. S. (1980). Response-shift bias a problem in evaluating interventions with pre/post self-reports. *Evaluation Review, 4*(1), 93-106.

Jastreboff, M. M., & Jastreboff, P. J. (2002). Decreased sound tolerance and tinnitus retraining therapy (TRT). *Australian and New Zealand Journal of Audiology, 24*(2), 74-84. doi:10.1375/audi.24.2.74.3110

Jastreboff, M.M., & Jastreboff, P.J. (2014). Treatments for decreased sound tolerance (hyperacusis and misophonia). *Seminars in Hearing 35*(2), 105-120. doi: 10.1055/s-0034-1372527

Johnson, M. (2014, February). *50 cases of misophonia using the MMP*. Paper presented at the misophonia conference of the Tinnitus Practitioners Association, Atlanta, GA.

Johnson, P. L., Webber, T. A., Wu, M. S., Lewin, A. B., Murphy, T. K., & Storch, E. A. (2013). When selective audiovisual stimuli become unbearable: A case series on pediatric misophonia. *Neuropsychiatry, 3*(6), 569-575.

Kumar, S., Hancock, O., Cope, T., Sedley, W., Winston, J., & Griffiths, T. D. (2014). Misophonia: A disorder of emotion processing of sounds. *Journal of Neurology, Neurosurgery, and Psychiatry*, 85(8):e3. doi: 10.1136/jnnp-2014-308883.38.

Lattal, K. M. (2012). Pavlovian conditioning. In G.J. Madden (Ed.), *APA handbook of behavior analysis: vol. 1 methods and principles* (pp. 283-306). Washington, DC: American Psychological Association Press.

Lehrer, P. M., Woolfolk, R. L., Rooney, A. J., McCann, B., & Carrington, P. (1983). Progressive relaxation and meditation: A study of psychophysiological and therapeutic differences between two techniques. *Behaviour Research and Therapy, 21*(6), 651-662. doi:10.1016/0005-7967(83)90083-9

Martz, K. (2013). *Patient Panel.* Presentation at the annual conference of the Misophonia Association, Portland, OR.

McGuire, J.F., Wu, M.S., & Storch, E.A. (2015). Cognitive Behavioral Therapy for Two Youth with Misophonia. *Journal of Clinical Psychiatry.*

Møller, A. R. (2011). Misophonia, phonophobia, and "exploding head" syndrome. In A. R. Møller, B. Langguth, D. DeRidder, & T. Kleinjung, (Eds.), *Textbook of tinnitus* (pp. 25-27). NY: Springer Publishing.

O'Bannon, R. M., Richard, H. C., & Runcie, D. (1987). Progressive relaxation as a function of procedural variations and anxiety level. *International Journal of Psychophysiology, 5*(3), 207-214. doi:10.1016/0167-8760(87)90007-9

Öst, L. G. (1987). Applied relaxation: description of a coping technique and review of controlled studies. *Behaviour Research and Therapy, 25*(5), 397-409. doi:10.1016/0005-7967(87)90017-9

Öst, L. G. (1988a). Applied relaxation vs progressive relaxation in the treatment of panic disorder. *Behaviour Research and Therapy, 26*(1), 13-22. doi:10.1016/0005-7967(88)90029-0

Öst, L. G. (1988b). Applied relaxation: Description of an effective coping technique. *Cognitive Behaviour Therapy, 17*(2), 83-96. doi:10.1016/0005-7967(87)90017-9

Pavlov, I. P. (2003). *Conditioned Reflexes.* (V. G. Anrep, Trans.). Mineola, NY: Dover Publications. (Original work published 1927)

Rattaz, C., Goubet, N., & Bullinger, A. (2005). The calming effect of a familiar odor on full-term newborns. *Journal of Developmental & Behavioral Pediatrics 26*(2), 86-92. doi:10.1097/00004703-200504000-00003

Schröder, A., Vulink, N., & Denys, S. (2013). Misophonia: Diagnostic criteria for a new psychiatric disorder. *PLoS ONE 8*, e54706. doi: 10.1371/journal.pone.0054706

Ulrich, R. E., & Azrin, N. H. (1962). Reflexive fighting in response to aversive stimulation. *Journal of the Experimental Analysis of Behavior, 5*, 511-520. doi: 10.1901/jeab.1962.5-511

Van de Mortel, T. F. (2008). Faking it: social desirability response bias in self-report research. *The Australian Journal of Advanced Nursing, 25*(4), 40-48.

Wu, M. S., Lewin, A. B., Murphy, T. K. & Storch, E. A. (2014). Misophonia: Incidence, phenomenology, and clinical correlates in an undergraduate student sample. *Journal of Clinical Psychology, 70*(10),1-14. doi: 10.1002/jclp.22098

Zald, D. H., Lee, J. T., Fluegel, K. W., & Pardo, J. V. (1998). Aversive gustatory stimulation activates limbic circuits in humans. *Brain, 121*(6), 1143-1154. doi: http://dx.doi.org/10.1093/brain/121.6.1143

Zald, D. H., & Pardo, J. V. (1997). Emotion, olfaction, and the human amygdala: Amygdala activation during aversive olfactory stimulation. *Proceedings of the National Academy of Sciences, 9*(8), 4119-24.

Citations

[1] Jastreboff & Jastreboff, 2002

[2] Bernstein, Angell, & Dehle, 2013

[3] Bernstein, Angell, & Dehle, 2013; Dozier, 2015a; Johnson et al., 2013; Schröder, Vulink, & Denys, 2013

[4] Schröder, Vulink, & Denys, 2013

[5] Schröder, Vulink, & Denys, 2013
Note: This form has been modified by replacing "sounds" with "triggers" to include visual and sound triggers.

[6] Johnson, 2014

[7] Dozier, 2014

[8] Wu, Lewin, Murphy, & Storch, 2014

[9] Accessed from http://blog.23andme.com/23andme-research/something-to-chew-on/ on June 7, 2015

[10] Wu, Lewin, Murphy, & Storch, 2014

[11] Bernstein, Angell, & Dehle, 2013; Edelstein, Brang, Rouw, & Ramachandran, 2013; Jastreboff & Jastreboff, 2014; Kumar et al., 2014; Schröder, Vulink, & Denys, 2013; Webber & Storch, 2015; Wu, Lewin, Murphy, & Storch, 2014

[12] Berkowitz, Cochran, & Embree, 1981; Berkowitz, 1983

[13] Zald & Pardo, 1997; Zald, Lee, Fluegel, & Pardo, 1998

[14] Ulrich & Azrin, 1962

[15] Lattal, 2012; Pavlov, 2003

[16] Goubet, Strasbauch, & Chesney, 2007; Rattaz, Goubet, & Bullinger, 2005

[17] Pavlov, 2003

[18] Donahoe & Vegas, 2004

[19] Furedy & Riley, 1987

[20] Wu, Lewin, Murphy, & Storch, 2014; Fayzullina et al., 2015

[21] Dozier, 2015b

[22] Donahoe & Vegas, 2004

[23] Johnson, 2014

[24] Johnson, 2014

[25] Borkovec & Sides, 1979

[26] Borkovec & Sides, 1979; Lehrer, Woolfolk, Rooney, McCann, & Carrington, 1983; O'Bannon, Richard, & Runcie, 1987

[27] Bourne, 2011

[28] Borkovec & Sides, 1979; Conrad & Roth, 2007; Dehghan-Nayeri & Adib-Hajbaghery, 2011; O'Bannon, Richard, & Runcie, 1987; Öst, 1987, 1988a

[29] Conrad, & Roth, 2007; Öst, 1987, 1988b

[30] Öst, L. G. 1988.

[31] Bourne, 2011

[32] Martz, 2013

[33] Dozier, in press

[34] Bernstein, Angell, & Dehle, 2013

[35] McGuare, Wu, & Storch, 2015

[36] http://www.randallrlylephd.com/ accessed on June 4, 2015

[37] Jastreboff & Jastreboff, 2014.

[38] Howard, 1980; Van de Mortel, 2008

[39] Schröder, Vulink, & Denys, 2013

[40] Møller, 2011

[41] Wu, Lewin, Murphy, & Storch, 2014

[42] Schröder, Vulink, & Denys, 2013

CPSIA information can be obtained
at www.ICGtesting.com
Printed in the USA
FSOW02n0007050815
9384FS